Campaign

OSPREY
PUBLISHING

Marston Moor 1644

The beginning of the end

OSPREY
PUBLISHING

Marston Moor 1644

The beginning of the end

John Tincey · Illustrated by Graham Turner

Series editor Lee Johnson · Consultant editor David G Chandler

First published in Great Britain in 2003 by Osprey Publishing, Elms Court,
Chapel Way, Botley, Oxford OX2 9LP, United Kingdom.
Email: info@ospreypublishing.com

A CIP catalogue record for this book is available from the British Library

ISBN 1 84176 334 9

Editor: Lee Johnson
Design: The Black Spot
Index by David Worthington
Maps by The Map Studio
3D bird's-eye views by The Black Spot
Battlescene artwork by Graham Turner

Originated by The Electronic Page Company, Cwmbran, UK
Printed in China through World Print Ltd.

03 04 05 06 07   10 9 8 7 6 5 4 3 2 1

For a catalogue of all books published by Osprey Military
and Aviation please contact:

The Marketing Manager, Osprey Direct UK,
PO Box 140, Wellingborough, Northants,
NN8 4ZA, United Kingdom.
Email: info@ospreydirect.co.uk

The Marketing Manager, Osprey Direct USA,
c/o Motorbooks International, PO Box 1,
Osceola, WI 54020-0001, USA.
Email: info@ospreydirectusa.com

www.ospreypublishing.com

Author's note

All pictures in this volume that are not specifically credited
are from the author's collection.

Artist's note

Readers may care to note that the original paintings from
which the colour plates in this book were prepared are
available for private sale. All reproduction copyright
whatsoever is retained by the Publishers. All enquiries
should be addressed to:

Graham Turner
'Five Acres'
Buslins Lane,
Chartridge, Chesham,
Bucks, HP5 2SN
UK

The Publishers regret that they can enter into no
correspondence upon this matter.

KEY TO MILITARY SYMBOLS

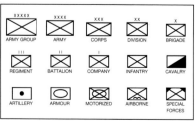

CONTENTS

THE OPENING CAMPAIGNS OF 1644

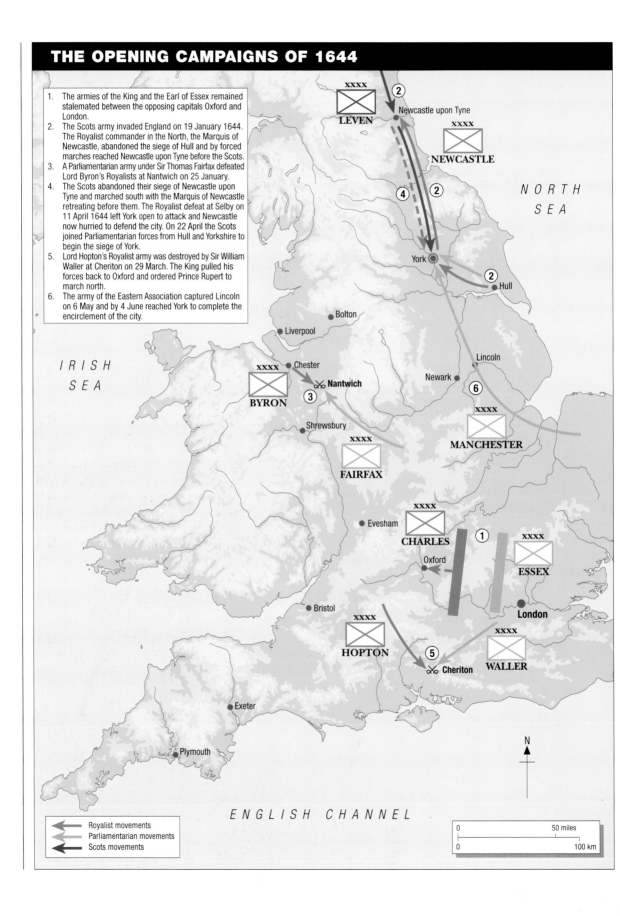

1. The armies of the King and the Earl of Essex remained stalemated between the opposing capitals Oxford and London.
2. The Scots army invaded England on 19 January 1644. The Royalist commander in the North, the Marquis of Newcastle, abandoned the siege of Hull and by forced marches reached Newcastle upon Tyne before the Scots.
3. A Parliamentarian army under Sir Thomas Fairfax defeated Lord Byron's Royalists at Nantwich on 25 January.
4. The Scots abandoned their siege of Newcastle upon Tyne and marched south with the Marquis of Newcastle retreating before them. The Royalist defeat at Selby on 11 April 1644 left York open to attack and Newcastle now hurried to defend the city. On 22 April the Scots joined Parliamentarian forces from Hull and Yorkshire to begin the siege of York.
5. Lord Hopton's Royalist army was destroyed by Sir William Waller at Cheriton on 29 March. The King pulled his forces back to Oxford and ordered Prince Rupert to march north.
6. The army of the Eastern Association captured Lincoln on 6 May and by 4 June reached York to complete the encirclement of the city.

LEVEN

Newcastle upon Tyne

NEWCASTLE

NORTH SEA

York

Hull

IRISH SEA

Bolton

Liverpool

Lincoln

Chester

BYRON

Nantwich

Newark

Shrewsbury

FAIRFAX

MANCHESTER

Evesham

CHARLES

Oxford

ESSEX

Bristol

London

HOPTON

Cheriton

WALLER

Exeter

Plymouth

ENGLISH CHANNEL

N

Royalist movements
Parliamentarian movements
Scots movements

0		50 miles
0		100 km

INTRODUCTION –
THE EVENTS OF 1644

For Charles I the new year of 1644 held out every prospect of victory over his rebellious Parliament. The old year of 1643 had closed with his armies holding the upper hand in every theatre of war. In the southern counties the Parliamentarian army of Sir William Waller had been all but annihilated at Roundway Down on 13 July 1643. In the West 13 days later, Prince Rupert had accepted the surrender of Bristol, a major seaport and the second city in the kingdom.

The King's own campaigning had not met with great success. The siege of Gloucester had been abandoned in the face of a relieving Parliamentarian army led by the Earl of Essex. Having cut Essex's line of retreat to London, the King had failed to capitalise on his advantage at the first battle of Newbury[1] (20 September 1643) and the Parliamentarians had marched back to London to a heroes' welcome. However the King's army once again threatened London and his cavalry had confirmed their marked superiority on the battlefield.

In the North the victories of 1643 appeared decisive. The Royalist army of the Marquis of Newcastle had defeated the Parliamentarians at Adwalton Moor on 30 June 1643 and had besieged the forces of Lord Fairfax in Hull. The latter's son, Sir Thomas Fairfax, had been driven into East Anglia, where a junior Parliamentarian commander named Oliver Cromwell had triumphed in a minor action at Gainsborough on 28 July 1643. Fairfax and Cromwell united their forces to achieve another success at Winceby on 11 September 1643.

---

1 See Campaign 116 *First Newbury 1643*.

Hollar's map of the Newcastle upon Tyne region reflects the rugged and hilly nature of the countryside that proved a check to the use of the superior Royalist Horse.

Alexander Leslie, Earl of Leven, a veteran of the Swedish service, was the senior Allied commander at Marston Moor. His victory was marred by his flight from the battlefield when all seemed lost following the defeat of the Allied right wing.

In the North West of England the King could hope for rapid progress. In November 1643 five regiments of 'Irish' Foot soldiers arrived in Cheshire. These were in fact English soldiers freed from service in Ireland by a cessation of the rebellion that had formed a separate war in that kingdom since 1641. A further seven regiments of Foot and one of Horse were to follow.

It came as a shock to the Royalist cause when the first engagement of 1644 saw them suffer a serious defeat in the North West. Having been driven from their native Yorkshire into East Anglia, the forces of Sir Thomas Fairfax were free to march to Cheshire to the relief of the Parliamentarian garrison at Nantwich. On 25 January 1644, Fairfax fell on the besieging Royalist forces of Lord Byron, which were divided by a river, and defeated them in detail. Fairfax and Lord Byron would each command the right wing cavalry of their respective army at Marston Moor.

This Parliamentarian victory in the North West would have been of little consequence but for events occurring in the North East. Parliament had felt the full force of the Royalist victories of 1643 and had resorted to desperate measures. Scotland, which like Ireland was

ABOVE **The Earl of Manchester was appointed to command the army of the Eastern Association because of his political influence.**

RIGHT **Sir Thomas Fairfax provided military ability in support of his father, Lord Fairfax. Despite the defeat of his right wing cavalry at Marston Moor, Sir Thomas remained on the field and his reputation remained untarnished.**

ruled by Charles I as a separate kingdom, had been first to rebel against the King and to establish a government based upon the Presbyterian form of Protestantism. On 23 November 1643, Parliament agreed that England would adopt Presbyterianism in return for the support of a Scots army of 18,000 Foot, 3,000 Horse and 120 cannon. On 19 January 1644 this army crossed the River Tweed and began an advance into the Marquis of Newcastle's recruiting grounds. Newcastle's army had been wintering in its siege lines before Hull. Now he led it in a desperate race to beat the Scots to the vital town of Newcastle upon Tyne. The Scots army arrived before the town on 3 February, but the leading regiments of Newcastle's army had arrived 12 hours earlier.

On 19 February the Scots clashed with a Royalist force commanded by Sir Marmaduke Langdale at Corbridge and suffered a sharp defeat. Alexander Leslie, Earl of Leven, quickly learned the lesson that his raw cavalry could not match the veteran Royalist Horse and that he must avoid battle in terrain suitable for cavalry fighting.

The hardship of the winter siege of Newcastle upon Tyne soon convinced Leven that to survive his army must march further into England in search of supplies. Leaving the town still defiant the Scots marched south with the Royalists shadowing them. On two occasions the armies clashed in country that did not allow the cavalry to become engaged. The Royalists fell back to Durham and the Scots drew close to that city but made no assault.

THE SIEGE OF YORK, 22 APRIL–1 JULY 1644

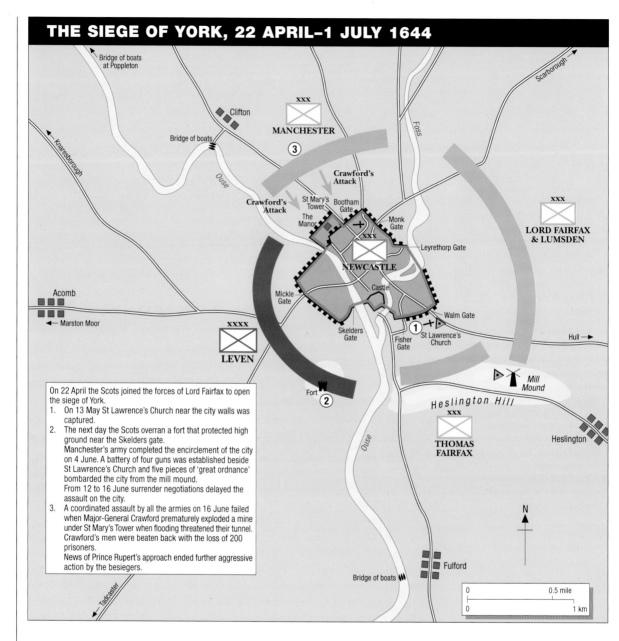

On 22 April the Scots joined the forces of Lord Fairfax to open the siege of York.

1. On 13 May St Lawrence's Church near the city walls was captured.
2. The next day the Scots overran a fort that protected high ground near the Skelders gate.
   Manchester's army completed the encirclement of the city on 4 June. A battery of four guns was established beside St Lawrence's Church and five pieces of 'great ordnance' bombarded the city from the mill mound.
   From 12 to 16 June surrender negotiations delayed the assault on the city.
3. A coordinated assault by all the armies on 16 June failed when Major-General Crawford prematurely exploded a mine under St Mary's Tower when flooding threatened their tunnel. Crawford's men were beaten back with the loss of 200 prisoners.
   News of Prince Rupert's approach ended further aggressive action by the besiegers.

On 12 April the Marquis of Newcastle received news that John Belasyse, Royalist governor of York, had suffered a disastrous defeat at the hands of Sir Thomas Fairfax. At Selby near York Belasyse had been captured and a large part of York's garrison routed. After his victory at Nantwich Fairfax had returned to his native Yorkshire. Newcastle's abandonment of the siege of Hull to counter the Scots invasion allowed Sir Thomas to join forces with the garrison of Hull, commanded by Lord Fairfax.

Newcastle now force-marched to reinforce York before the victorious Parliamentarians overwhelmed the depleted garrison. During the march south his Foot regiments lost many stragglers and deserters, further reducing his battered army. On 14 and 15 April his regiments staggered into York and on 18 April the Scots made contact with the Parliamentarian forces of Sir Thomas Fairfax. York was now in a state of siege.

CHRONOLOGY

1644

19 January Scots army invades England in support of the Parliament.

25 January Battle of Nantwich.

3 February Scots begin the siege of Newcastle upon Tyne.

6 February Prince Rupert is appointed to command Royalist forces in northern England.

19 February Scots cavalry defeated in skirmish at Corbridge.

21 March Rupert relieves Newark.

29 March Battle of Cheriton.

11 April Yorkshire Royalists defeated at Selby.

14 April Marquis of Newcastle reaches York.

18 April Scots join with Fairfax to begin the siege of York.

25 April Rupert returns to Oxford.

5 May Rupert leaves Oxford for the North.

28 May Rupert storms Bolton.

30 May Royalist cavalry from York join forces with Rupert.

3 June Army of the Eastern Association joins the Allied army to complete the encirclement of York.

6 June The King's army reaches Worcester.

6 June The Parliamentarian army of the Earl of Essex marches south leaving the army of Sir William Waller to watch the King.

11 June The King writes to Rupert proposing the relief of York.

14 June The King writes to Rupert ordering him to relieve York and to defeat the Scots.

15 June The King's army evades Waller and marches for Oxford.

16 June Allied assault on York fails.

18 June The King's army is reunited outside Oxford.

20 June Waller arrives at Gloucester still seeking the King's army in the Severn Valley.

26 June Rupert at Skipton Castle.

28 June Allied commanders at York are warned of Rupert's approach.

28 June Waller reaches Banbury within striking distance of the King's army.

29 June Battle of Cropredy Bridge.

1 July Royalist cavalry approach York from the direction of Knaresborough.

1 July Rupert's main army reaches the outskirts of York relieving the city.

2 July BATTLE OF MARSTON MOOR.

3 July The King at Evesham receives reports of a victory at York, but news of the defeat quickly follows and he determines to march for Exeter to join the Queen.

18 July The Earl of Essex relieves the Parliamentarian garrison of Plymouth.

26 July Sir William Waller arrives in London, his army in a state of mutiny.

14 August Parliamentary cavalry sent to reinforce Essex are defeated at Bridgewater.

21 August Essex's army is cut off and his infantry forced to surrender at Lostwithiel.

30 September The King and Rupert meet for the first time following Marston Moor.

2 October The King's army threatens Parliamentarian positions in Dorset.

18 October Parliamentarian armies assemble at Basingstoke.

27 October Second battle of Newbury.

9 November The King's army returns to Donnington Castle, near Newbury, to recover its wounded and artillery. The Parliamentarians refuse to give battle.

19 December The Self-Denying Ordinance is passed by the House of Commons. It stipulates that no member of the House of Commons or House of Lords can hold a command in the army or navy.

1645

3 April After some delay, the House of Lords pass the Self-Denying Ordinance.

OPPOSING COMMANDERS

ALLIED COMMANDERS

Alexander Leslie, First Earl of Leven, (1582–1661) entered military service with the Dutch in 1605. In 1608 he transferred to the Swedish service and over the next 20 years rose to the rank of colonel. In 1628 Leslie made his name with an energetic defence of the town of Stralsund, forcing the Imperialists, under the renowned Count Wallenstein, to abandon the siege. He briefly returned to Scotland in 1635, before being called to support the Swedish General Johan Baner in his victory at Wittstock.

In October 1638 Leslie returned to Scotland where the profits of campaigning had purchased two earldoms. He found Scotland in a tumult of opposition to the religious reforms of King Charles. Leslie sided with the Covenanters, who appointed him to lead their fledgling army. The collapse of the English military preparations forced King Charles into a humiliating peace in 1639. The following year the King resumed military preparations against the Scots but Leslie struck first, defeating an English force at Newburn and capturing Newcastle upon Tyne.

Leslie was the unquestioned choice to command the Scots army sent to the aid of Parliament under the Solemn League and Covenant in 1644.

Edward Montagu, second Earl of Manchester, (1602–1671) served as Member of Parliament for Huntingdon until 1626 when he was elevated to the House of Lords as Baron Montagu of Kimbolton. When his father became first Earl of Manchester, Montagu gained the courtesy title of Viscount Mandeville.

Montagu married the daughter of the Earl of Warwick, the future admiral of Parliament's fleet and brother of the Earl of Essex, Parliament's future Lord General. Montagu was a natural member of the 'Puritan' faction in the House of Lords and an opponent to the Royalist majority.

Montagu served with the Dutch Army and took part in the war against the Scots, but his political opposition to the King increased as civil war drew near and he was linked with the 'five members' accused by the King of treason.

In November 1642 Montagu became the second Earl of Manchester on the death of his father. In August 1643 he was commissioned as Major-General of the forces of the Eastern Association, with Oliver Cromwell appointed as the commander of the Horse.

Montagu proved an unenthusiastic commander. In August 1643 he set about the capture of King's Lynn, which had been seized by Royalists. The town fell on 16 September and Montagu moved on to besiege Bolingbroke Castle, occasioning the battle at Winceby on 11 October. On 20 October Lincoln fell and Montagu returned to London. Lincoln was recaptured by the Royalists and it was not until 6 May 1644 that the city again fell to the army of the Eastern Association, which was at last free to march towards York.

Sir Thomas Fairfax (1612–1671) was born on the family estate at Denton, near Ilkley, in the West Riding of Yorkshire. His father succeeded to the title of Baron Fairfax of Cameron in the Scottish peerage in 1640.

Thomas Fairfax's military career began when at 17 he entered the Dutch service under Sir Horace Vere. Fairfax was knighted for his service against the Scots in 1640, but when civil war approached in England he sided with Parliament. When King Charles called the Yorkshire gentry to a gathering at Heyworth Moor in June 1642, Fairfax attempted to present him with a petition from the pro-Parliamentarian gentry of Yorkshire. The King refused to accept the petition and brushed Fairfax aside.

During 1643 the Fairfaxes, father and son, fought a difficult defensive campaign against the superior forces of the Marquis of Newcastle until their eventual defeat at Adwalton Moor on 30 June 1643. Lord Fairfax retired to the Parliamentarian stronghold of Hull while Sir Thomas slipped across the River Humber with his cavalry to join forces with Oliver Cromwell.

In early 1644 he was sent north to Cheshire to the relief of Nantwich where he crushed the Royalist army of Lord Byron. The distraction of Newcastle's army by the Scots invasion enabled Fairfax to re-enter his native Yorkshire and to rejoin his father to begin the campaign that would end at Marston Moor.

Oliver Cromwell (1599–1658) was raised as a poor relation to his uncle Sir Hugh Cromwell of Hinchingbrook. He was a member of the lowest level of the minor gentry. Financial problems had brought him to the ungentlemanly expedient of labouring in his own fields. Saved from social disgrace and mental collapse by a religious conversion, Cromwell began to make contacts amongst the influential Puritan families of East Anglia and London. His career as Member of Parliament for Huntingdon was cut short when King Charles dismissed his Parliament and set out on an 11-year personal rule. In 1640 defeat in his war against the Scots required the King to recall Parliament and Cromwell was elected as member for Cambridge. In the pre-war manoeuvrings of 1642 he became a minor public hero by preventing the Cambridge colleges from sending their plate to swell the King's coffers.

At Edgehill in 1642[2], Cromwell commanded a troop of Horse but arrived only to fight at the end of the battle. Early in 1643 Cromwell returned to East Anglia with the rank of colonel to raise a regiment of Horse. At Grantham on 13 May 1643 with 12 troops of Horse, 'some so poor and broken that you shalt seldom see worse', Cromwell encountered a Royalist force of twice his size. Cromwell chose his moment and with a controlled charge, at the trot, scattered his opponents.

At Gainsborough on 20 July 1643, Cromwell took his troopers across broken ground to face and defeat a body of Royalist Horse in a strong defensive position. A general pursuit ensued but Cromwell had kept three reserve troops under his command and was able to defeat a Royalist counter-attack.

Ferdinando, Lord Fairfax was the leader of the Parliamentarian forces in Yorkshire, but he was heavily dependent upon the military skill of his son, Sir Thomas.

We are accustomed to portraits of Cromwell as Lord Protector, but he was not always so well known.

In this group portrait of Parliamentarian generals Cromwell is barely recognisable, but his placement next to the Earl of Essex marks him as a man of growing importance.

In August 1643 Parliament appointed Cromwell to command the cavalry of the army of the Eastern Association under the Earl of Manchester. On 11 October Cromwell encountered a force of Royalist Horse at Winceby. Cromwell's horse was shot from under him and he was knocked to the ground by a Royalist trooper. Fortunately he sustained only minor injuries and was able to remount to rejoin the fighting that, following a charge led by Sir Thomas Fairfax, resulted in a Parliamentarian victory.

On 21 January 1644 Cromwell received a commission as a Lieutenant-General, and in February he became a member of the Committee of Both Kingdoms, the combined Scots and Parliamentarian war council. He was now also the only Parliamentarian commander of note who remained undefeated in action against the Royalist Horse.

ROYALIST COMMANDERS

Prince Rupert of the Rhine (1619–1682), son of Frederick, Elector Palatine, and King Charles's sister Elizabeth, spent his childhood in Holland. His father had lost his hereditary estates after he was deposed as elected King of Bohemia following the battle of the White Mountain (1620) early in the Thirty Years War.

At the age of 14 Rupert joined the Dutch army at the siege of Rheinberg in 1633. He fought at the siege of Breda in 1637 and was captured fighting under Swedish command at Lemgo in 1638 in the course of a heroic cavalry charge which General James King, the future Lord Eythin, failed to support.

During his three-year captivity in Linz and Vienna, Rupert was able to make a wide-ranging study of military practice on a theoretical level. Rupert's staunch Protestantism prevented him from accepting the commands he was offered by Europe's Catholic monarchs. The outbreak of war in England allowed Rupert to resume his military career while honouring the condition of his release that he would never fight against the Emperor.

King Charles appointed Rupert General of Horse with the privilege of taking orders only from the King himself. This curious arrangement caused problems when Rupert interfered in the formations used by the Royalist Foot at Edgehill, causing the Earl of Lindsey, the Lord General, to withdraw from command to fight at the head of his own regiment. Rupert's outdated Swedish Brigade formation proved too complex for the inexperienced Royalist Foot, contributing to their defeat. Fortunately the success of Rupert's cavalry saved the Royalists from defeat at Edgehill and established his reputation for invincibility with friend and foe alike.

In an engraving which depicts Royalist leaders drowning in a stormy sea, Cromwell is chosen as one of the Parliamentarian commanders meriting an individual portrait.

Created an Earl in 1628 by King Charles, **William Cavendish, Marquis of Newcastle** (1592–1676) had obtained the post of Governor to the Prince of Wales. His connections with the Stuart household made him a natural Royalist when civil war broke out. Newcastle was appointed General of the King's forces north of the River Trent and before the outbreak of hostilities had secured Newcastle upon Tyne and raised a small army that he used to secure the city of York.

During 1643, Newcastle laboriously pushed the Parliamentarians out of Yorkshire until they held only the port of Hull. Encouraged by the King to march on London, Newcastle reached no further than Lincolnshire before returning to York, claiming that his officers would march no further with Hull defiant at their backs. Newcastle's siege of Hull was a humiliating failure and he was forced to withdraw leaving many of his cannon stuck in the waterlogged trenches. The entry of the Scots into the war, on the side of Parliament, forced Newcastle onto the defensive for the remainder of his short military career. In the aftermath of the defeat at Marston Moor he abandoned the Royalist cause and fled into foreign exile.

Lord John Byron, first Baron of Rochdale (d. 1652) was the eldest son of Sir John Byron of Newstead Abbey in Nottinghamshire and sat as Member of Parliament for the county until 1628. He saw service in the Dutch army and took part in the war against the Scots in 1640. From December 1641 to February 1642 Byron held the Lieutenancy of the Tower of London and began to fortify it for the King until Parliament became aware of his activities and demanded his removal. In his response to the King, Byron added his own pleas for release from the troubles of the Lieutenancy.

Byron was one of the first to rally to the King and he was present at the abortive attempt on Coventry in August 1642. Sent with a convoy of valuables to Oxford, Byron was ambushed near Brackley on 28 August 1642 and Parliamentarian propagandists claimed that he lost between £6,000 and £8,000.

Cromwell is singled out for praise as 'Religious successful and truly Valliant' in this propaganda portrait.

Prince Rupert gained valuable experience in European wars and as the King's nephew was able to achieve high command at the early age of 23.

This did not deter Byron from successfully shipping the contributions of the University of Oxford to Worcester where he was relieved by Prince Rupert, leading to the first significant military clash of the war at Powick Bridge.

At Edgehill, Byron commanded Rupert's second line and failed to keep these reserves under control. In his defence few other Royalist commanders succeeded where he failed. On 13 July 1643 Byron scored a signal success in a charge that destroyed the cuirassier regiment of Sir Arthur Haslerigge at the battle of Roundway Down. Byron next commanded a wing of the Royalist Horse in the confused hedge fighting at Newbury on 20 September 1643 and was rewarded with elevation to Baron Byron of Rochdale.

Byron conspired to obtain an independent command in Lancashire and was reinforced by regiments from Ireland freed by the King's treaty with the Confederate rebels. With this new strength Byron drove the Parliamentarians back to their last garrison of Nantwich. A relieving force under the command of Sir Thomas Fairfax took the opportunity to rout Byron's divided army when a sudden thaw washed away the bridge linking the two parts of the besieging Royalist force.

Byron withdrew to Chester to await the arrival of Prince Rupert. The behaviour and ill discipline of his troops damaged Byron's reputation, while an incident in which prisoners were massacred at Barthomley Church gave him the nickname of 'Bloody Braggadochio Byron' and served to justify reprisals by Parliamentarians against his 'Irish' soldiers for years to come.

Sir Richard Bulstrode, secretary to **Lord George Goring** (1620–1657), wrote: 'he strangely loved the bottle, was much given to his pleasures and a great debauchee.' Heir to a baronetcy and son-in-law to the millionaire Earl of Cork, Goring nevertheless found himself short of money in 1633 and he entered the Dutch service on the recommendation of Strafford, the Lord Deputy of Ireland. Goring's social connections brought him the rank of colonel. However, he soon showed a talent for command and great personal bravery. At the siege of Breda in 1637 a musket ball shattered his ankle as he worked alongside his men in a trench under enemy fire. The constant pain from this injury may have been a cause of his alcoholism.

Goring served in both Bishops Wars against the Scots and was appointed Governor of the vital port of Portsmouth in the approach to civil war. In 1641 a group of officers conspired in the 'Army Plot' to threaten Parliament. Goring argued that the officers should march on the Tower of London to free Strafford, who was held there under threat of death. Finding his proposals rejected, Goring related the conspiracy to his friend Lord Newport who, as Goring perhaps intended, passed word to the leaders of Parliament.

Some of the conspirators were arrested but Goring convinced Parliament of his loyalty and retained the Governorship of Portsmouth. In 1642 Goring was appointed Lieutenant-General to the Earl of Essex but declared for the King in August of that year. Portsmouth could not hope for relief from the King and after a brief siege Goring sailed to join the Queen in Holland.

Returning to Northern England in 1643 Goring was appointed General of Horse to the Marquis of Newcastle and defeated Fairfax at Seacroft Moor. Fairfax then captured Goring while he lay sick with fever when Wakefield fell to the Parliamentarians.

Exchanged after nine months' captivity, in April 1644 Goring joined Prince Rupert at Preston where he took command of Newcastle's Horse, which were serving with Rupert.

OPPOSING ARMIES

Five independent armies assembled on Marston Moor.

The Royalist Army of Prince Rupert

Rupert brought his own regiment of Foot, his regiment of Horse and his Lifeguard of Horse with him into the North. He incorporated the remains of Lord Byron's Horse and Foot into his army, including regiments arrived from Ireland, and raised fresh contingents from Lancashire, Cumberland, Staffordshire and Derbyshire. Rupert may have amassed a force as large as 2,000 Horse and 6,000 Foot for the relief of York and he was able to add perhaps 5,000 Horse and 800 Foot of Newcastle's army, these having been sent out of the besieged city in order to reinforce him.

The Royalist Army of the Marquis of Newcastle

Newcastle's army had begun mustering before the formal outbreak of war, relying largely on the efforts of local worthies to recruit their servants and tenants to form troops and regiments. As Newcastle's army advanced into Parliamentarian-held areas more Royalist gentry came forward to raise new units. The disadvantage was that as the months of campaigning took their toll, existing regiments declined in strength as casualties were suffered but not replaced. Peter Young lists 45 regiments of Horse that may have been represented at Marston Moor. Given that Goring commanded the 5,000 Horse of Newcastle's army, many of the regiments must have been absent or have been reduced to the strength of a strong troop. Newcastle's Foot, amounting to 3,000 soldiers, was drawn up in seven divisions constituted by combining numerous smaller regiments. The Royalists may have had between 16 and 20 pieces of artillery on the battlefield, most of them light field pieces.

King Charles's sister Elizabeth, known as the Winter Queen, married the Elector Palatine and was the mother of Prince Rupert and Prince Maurice. When her husband was deposed as King of Bohemia in 1620, Elizabeth and her sons made a dramatic flight into exile and she became a Protestant heroine.

The Scots Army

The Scots gained experience of raising and maintaining armies during the Bishops Wars of 1639 and 1640 and from then until the arrival of Royalist forces under the Marquis of Montrose in mid-1644, had a united nation untroubled by war on which to base their operations. The Scots were strong in infantry and artillery, but their cavalry suffered from Scotland's inability to breed suitable horses in sufficient numbers. This marked inferiority to Newcastle's Horse severely limited the effectiveness of the Scots and slowed their advance into England.

The Scots entered England with 18,000 Foot, 3,000 Horse and 400 to 600 Dragoons. Lord Fairfax reported that this had fallen to 14,000 Foot and 2,000 Horse by the time the Scots reached York and numbers may have fallen further by the time of Marston Moor.

The Parliamentarian Army of Ferdinando Lord Fairfax

The army commanded by Lord Fairfax suffered a devastating defeat at Adwalton Moor in June 1643 that all but destroyed it as a fighting army. The Foot regiments retired into garrisons such as Hull and Sir Thomas Fairfax took the remnants of the Horse to the Eastern Association. Sir Thomas achieved a decisive victory at Nantwich in January 1644 and brought Lancashire forces with him to unite with those of his father, which took the field once more when Newcastle hurried north to meet the Scots. It is reported that Fairfax could contribute 3,000 Foot and 2,000 Horse to join Manchester after York had fallen. Sir Thomas Fairfax reported the joint forces of his father and the Scots to be 16,000 Foot and 4,000 Horse.

The Parliamentarian Army of the Eastern Association

The Earl of Manchester was appointed to command the army of the Eastern Association in August 1643 and he was able to draw on a number of regiments already active in the defence of the region. East Anglia provided a prosperous, strongly Parliamentarian base for the new army and the steady provision of pay and supplies enabled regiments to maintain their numbers of soldiers under arms to a degree that eluded most civil war commanders. Some 4,000 Horse and 4,000 Foot of Manchester's army may have been present at Marston Moor, marking them as the best balanced of the forces in the opinion of contemporary military theorists.

DEPLOYMENT

In addition to the information contained in the contemporary accounts of Marston Moor, two maps giving details of the deployment have survived. One is amongst the collection of civil war battle plans drawn by Bernard de Gomme, who accompanied the Royal armies during their campaigns. It is not known when the maps were drawn and it is possible that they were based upon headquarters plans like that of Marston Moor that Prince Rupert showed to General King. The de Gomme map of Marston Moor shows Prince Rupert's dispositions in great detail but also depicts the first two lines of the Allied army as they might have been seen by an observer on the moor. If de Gomme was not an eyewitness to the battle he may have drawn from the recollection of Royalist combatants during the long years of exile before the Restoration.

The second plan was drawn up by the Scots Sergeant-Major-General James Lumsden who appended it to a letter which he wrote on 5 July 1644 from York. As an officer with primary responsibility for drawing up part if not all of the Allied army, Lumsden can be expected to have had good information as to unit strengths and where they intended to deploy.

The Allied Army

Scoutmaster General Lionel Watson of the Eastern Association wrote that the Allied left wing consisted of about 70 troops and Lumsden gives Cromwell 3,000 Horse and the Scot David Leslie 1,000. Cromwell commanded 36 troops and David Leslie 22. Lumsden mentions 500 Dragoons who may account for another nine 'troops' (Dragoons were formed into companies as they fought on foot), five under John Lilburne and four belonging to Hugh Fraser. The maps depict six divisions in the front line and Lumsden lists that on the left hand as Dragoons. Cromwell's division was 300 strong and based on de Gomme's apportionment of cornets this may have been twice the size of the other divisions. The second line was commanded by Vermuyden and consisted of five divisions (or six in the reconstruction by Peter Young), which may have been composed of the 22 troops of Vermuyden's, Fleetwood's and Manchester's Regiments. The third line was composed of three Scots regiments. Lumsden shows a body of 50 musketeers standing to the right of each division of Horse.

The right wing commanded by Sir Thomas Fairfax was arranged in a similar manner to that of the left wing. Watson gives Fairfax 80 troops. Of these 22 troops of Scots formed the third line and the 500 Dragoons that Lumsden shows on the right of Fairfax's front line may have contributed to Watson's total. Lumsden gives Fairfax 3000 Horse with 1,000 Scots Horse in support. Bodies of 50 musketeers alongside each division also helped support the right wing.

The cavalry of the Allied army had remained on Marston Moor so that only the Foot Brigades of the three armies had to re-form their lines of battle to encounter the Royalists. Watson says 'Our Foot being twenty eight Regiments, were disposed into twelve Brigades'. De Gomme shows Brigades each of two regiments and Lumsden appears to represent 14 Brigades.

De Gomme's map gives an impression of the first two lines of the Allied army, but he did not have access to the Allied headquarters plans and could not speak to Allied veterans of the battle. Sir James Lumsden

John, Lord Byron, commanded the Royalist right wing cavalry at Marston Moor and has received much of the blame for the Royalist defeat.

George, Lord Goring, earned a reputation as a hard drinker and a hard fighter.

drew a rough sketch map of the Allied dispositions at the bottom of the letter in which he gave an account of the battle. Interpretation of the Lumsden map is not without problems. Age has damaged some areas so that the original markings are lost. Peter Young published a reconstruction of the Lumsden map based on surviving markings and upon other contemporary evidence that literally fills in the gaps.

Unlike de Gomme, Lumsden was making a quick sketch and he may have fallen into the common error of not beginning his work using a scale that allowed him to get all of the formations onto the page. The left wing Horse occupy nearly half of the width of the paper whereas the Foot and the Right wing Horse are crammed into the remaining space. For example the 500 Dragoons on the left wing take up about twice the space of the 500 Dragoons on the right wing.

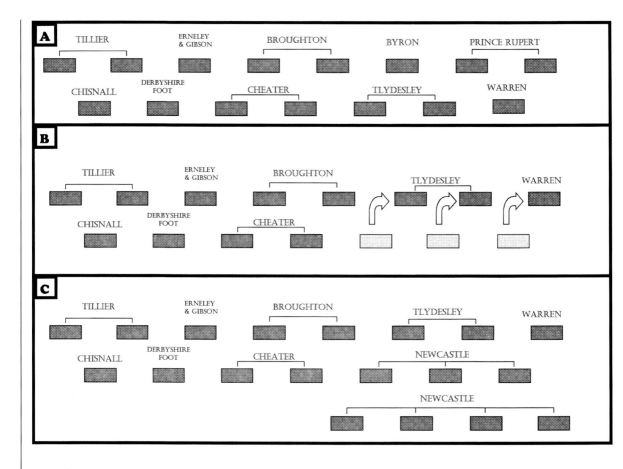

Taken together, the damaged page and the variable ground scale mean that Lumsden's map cannot be used in the same way as de Gomme's. Lumsden appears to have drawn the left wing Horse with six divisions (including one deduced by Peter Young) in the front line, which agrees with de Gomme's map. Peter Young inserts a small division in the second line based upon what may be a surviving corner of a unit on the edge of paper damage; this however places a division directly behind the division that Young introduced into the first line. Without Young's inserted division Lumsden shows five divisions in the second line covering the gaps in the first line, which agrees with de Gomme's map. De Gomme shows some divisions grouped in pairs or in three while Lumsden shows them covering a single gap. Young inserts another division, based upon a surviving corner, in the third line making four in total, although this line was reported to have comprised three Scots units.

Lumsden shows the third line standing immediately to the rear of the divisions in the second line. A debate at this time concerned the positioning of supporting cavalry. Some officers argued that when retiring Horse would wheel round to the rear, rather than individually about face as did the Foot. It therefore made little sense to have their supporting units standing in the rear in alignment with gaps between units in the front line, as a wheel to the rear would bring a retiring unit face to face with its supports. Where a third line of Horse was available it was usually positioned directly behind the second line to give first line units a clear line of retreat.

This diagrammatic representation offers a possible explanation for the deployment of the Royalist Foot at Marston Moor. 'A' depicts Rupert's Foot as it was originally drawn up. At 'B' Prince Rupert's and Byron's Regiments have marched away to support the artillery and second line units advance to take their places. At 'C' the first three divisions of Newcastle's Foot march into the gaps in the second line and the remainder of Newcastle's units fall in behind.

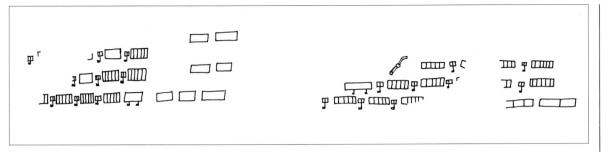

This drawing copies the surviving parts of the map drawn by Lumsden to indicate the dispositions of the Allied Army at Marston Moor. Damage to the paper has destroyed significant areas of the plan. Lumsden appears to follow the convention of the day of showing units of Horse (as opposed to Dragoons or Foot) as 'striped' or 'shaded' blocks.

Most, but not all, of the rectangles depicting Lumsden's divisions of Horse contain four lines drawn from front to back and it has been suggested that this is intended to depict that each body consisted of five troops. However such shading was a common indicator of Horse, as opposed to Foot or Dragoons, in the key used on headquarters maps.

Lumsden's effort at depicting the right wing Horse is much less detailed and more cramped. The units stand close together separated only by blocks of musketeers and are shown drawn up one behind the other. It may be that Lumsden did not have space to show the second line divisions covering the gaps in the first line and drew a representation of the units present rather than their exact dispositions.

De Gomme shows six divisions in each of the first two lines while Lumsden shows five in the first line and four in each of the second and third lines. However, paper damage may mean that some divisions on the far right wing have been lost from Lumsden's diagram.

Both de Gomme and Lumsden show a body of Dragoons on the left of the first line with supporting Horse directly behind in the second and third lines. This is a curious position as Dragoons did not fight mounted as part of the cavalry.

The Allied Foot

Lumsden's depiction of the Allied Foot has suffered greatly from both paper damage and lack of space. The key to his map implies five divisions in the front line, four in each of the second and third and a single division at the rear left forming the beginning of a fourth line. Unlike their cavalry the Allied Foot was forced to form up from the march and their order of marching had been reversed by their unexpected recall to Marston Moor. We know that the Scots marched in the van and that Manchester's brigades brought up the rear. De Gomme shows six Brigades in the first line and five in the second, each composed of two divisions.

The confusion in which the Allied Foot deployed makes it difficult to say with certainty that they would have followed normal practice. However, de Gomme's map shows the Allied Foot in the familiar chequerboard pattern of the second line covering gaps in the first line and Lumsden may not have intended an accurate representation of the deployment in his sketch for as he said in his letter 'the brigads drawen up heir ... not so formall as it ought to be'.

We know that the Scots had furthest to march back to Marston Moor so Scots brigades cannot initially have formed part of the first line. The second line was entirely composed of Scots brigades that cannot have moved into place before the brigades of Fairfax that formed the third line. It would seem reasonable that the brigades of Manchester's Foot,

This drawing copies the representation of the first two lines of the Allied army shown in De Gomme's map of the Royalist army. The top section shows Cromwell's left wing cavalry, the middle section the central infantry formation and the lower section Fairfax's right wing cavalry.

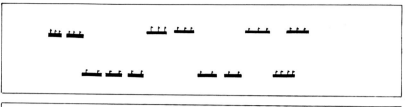

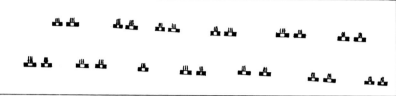

which had formed the rearguard that morning, arrived back first and formed up on the ridge. They were joined by Fairfax's Foot; the first brigade of Fairfax's Foot extending the front to the right of Manchester's brigades, already drawn up, and the others beginning a second line, with units drawing up level with the spaces in the first line.

The arrival of the Scots met with more confusion. Two brigades drew up on the right of the first line where a gap appears to have existed between Fairfax's Brigade and the right wing Horse. It may be that the Foot had moved to the left earlier in the day when Cromwell drove away Royalist Horse from the ridge and extended his Horse to the left to occupy the ground he had won. Manchester's Foot would be inclined to move to support their own Horse and to follow their movement to the left. Four Scots brigades now moved between the existing first and second lines to form a new second line. To achieve a balance a fifth brigade was required to complete the chequerboard effect in the newly arrived second line and the late-arriving brigade (shown as a solitary unit in the fourth line in Peter Young's reconstruction of Lumsden's map) may have been that of either Lord Sinclair's or Sir Patrick Hepburn's Regiment.

We have no plan of the placing of the artillery but Lumsden drew a cannon behind the left wing Horse and some Allied guns did manage to get into action before the main assault was launched.

The Royalist army

De Gomme's plan gives a great deal of information about the deployment of the Royalist armies but also raises a number of questions. The right wing Horse, under the command of Lord Byron, was drawn up in two lines. The first line, commanded by Byron in person, consisted of 11 divisions, grouped in three sets of three and one of two divisions. Each division of Horse had a unit of 50 musketeers stationed close behind it. The second line was commanded by Lord Molyneux and was made up of three bodies with two divisions in each. Prince Rupert's Regiment of Horse extended Molyneux's line to the left.

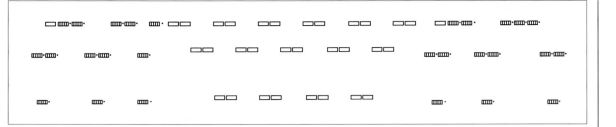

Byron's wing did not benefit from a natural feature on which to secure its flank. To defend the first line from an outflanking attack a regiment of 200 Horse under Sir Samuel Tuke was 'refused' by being positioned outside the body halfway between the first and second line.

Lord Goring commanded the left wing Horse. The first line was made up of two bodies with three divisions in each. Five divisions of Newcastle's Horse subsequently extended this line to the left. Six divisions in three bodies were drawn up to align with the gaps in the first line supported by a refused body of 200 Horse. The final unit of the second line and the refused body should have been aligned with the spaces in the first line but they were not. It is likely that the late arrival of front line units upset the deployment.

A brigade of Horse, under Sir William Blakiston, stood close behind the Foot. Rupert may have remembered the manner in which Parliamentarian Horse in a similar position had contributed to the defeat of the King's Foot at Edgehill.

The Horse regiment of Sir Edward Widdrington and Prince Rupert's Lifeguard of Horse stood as a central reserve.

A body of musketeers was drawn out to line the ditch and hedge that ran across the front of the Royalist army. This 'skirmish line' would have been of little use during a Royalist advance and is evidence that Rupert had amended his deployment to defend against an Allied attack.

The Royalist Foot

Historians have raised questions about the dispositions of the Royalist infantry at Marston Moor. The fundamental question is does de Gomme's map depict how the various units actually deployed, or is it merely a headquarters plan of where it was intended they should draw up with many, and in particular Newcastle's infantry, never reaching those positions? By detailed examination it is hoped to demonstrate that de Gomme accurately represents the Royalist dispositions at the start of the main fighting.

Military theory of the mid-17th century was based on a Dutch revival and adaptation of ancient Greek and Roman military practice. Armies were deployed according to a battle formation drawn up at the start of the campaign, with adjustments made on the day of battle to reflect the terrain and the forces actually available. In keeping with the revival of ancient learning, geometry, order and balance played a major part in the drawing up of these plans. For example the right and left wing cavalry formations of the Royalist army at Marston Moor can be seen to have begun as mirror images, with adjustments made for the units available on the day. Concepts of honour, rank and precedence of the colonel of a regiment also influenced where it stood in the line of battle.

Lumsden's sketch indicates the use of a chequerboard formation. This drawing shows a conjectural formation based on its use throughout the Allied armies, but a deployment that reconciles all the sources has not yet been devised.

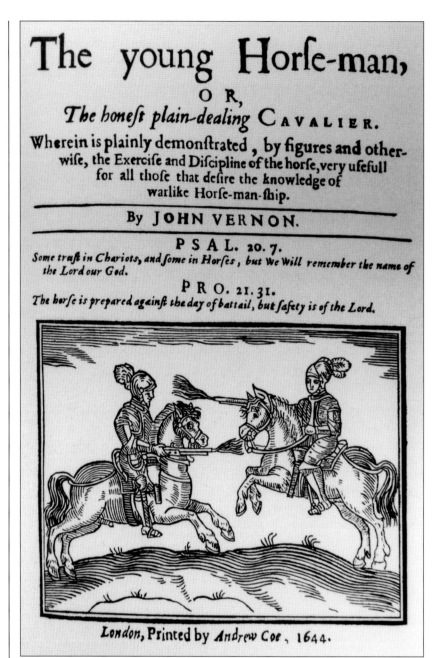

The young Horſe-man,
OR,
The honeſt plain-dealing CAVALIER.

Wherein is plainly demonſtrated, by figures and other-wiſe, the Exerciſe and Diſcipline of the horſe, very uſefull for all thoſe that deſire the knowledge of warlike Horſe-man-ſhip.

By JOHN VERNON.

PSAL. 20. 7.
Some traſt in Chariots, and ſome in Horſes, but We Will remember the name of the Lord our God.

PRO. 21. 31.
The horſe is prepared againſt the day of battail, but ſafety is of the Lord.

London, Printed by *Andrew Coe*, 1644.

John Vernon published his pamphlet on cavalry tactics in 1644. Serving with the Parliamentarian Army of the Earl of Essex, Vernon's advice gives us an insight into the way cavalry would have fought at Marston Moor.

The major areas of controversy that have arisen over the deployment of the Royalist Foot concern the seven divisions of Newcastle's infantry and the three divisions comprising Prince Rupert's and Lord Byron's regiments. The term division was used at this time to mean a body of soldiers.

Newcastle's men arrived late on the day of Marston Moor and formed up as the right hand three units of Rupert's second line, with their remaining four units drawn up to the rear of these. Historians have suggested that Rupert's battle plan and deployment left gaps in his line for Newcastle's infantry to occupy in the expectation that they would arrive early in the morning. If this was the case, why were Newcastle's regiments required to march over to the right of the second line given that they would be approaching from the left rear? Was Rupert such a negligent general that he would leave his army in the face of the enemy with its Foot in a half-completed formation until reinforcements arrived? The obvious answers to these questions suggest that Rupert did not deliberately draw up his Foot regiments with gaps in their formation awaiting Newcastle's arrival.

MILITARIE
INSTRUCTIONS
FOR THE
CAVALLRIE:
OR
RULES AND DIRECTIONS
FOR THE SERVICE OF
HORSE,

COLLECTED OUT OF DIVERS
FORRAIN AUTHORS ANCIENT
AND MODERN,

AND

RECTIFIED AND SUPPLIED, ACCORD-
ING TO THE PRESENT PRACTISE
OF THE LOW-COUNTREY
WARRES.

PROVERBS 21. 31.

The horse is prepared for battell: but victorie is from the Lord.

Printed by the printers to the UNIVERSITIE of CAMBRIDGE. MDCXXXII.

Vernon's pamphlet had a limited circulation. The standard work on cavalry was by John Cruso and it proved so successful that no other book dealing only with cavalry was published for a generation.

The hollow-Square girdled with shot.

Front.

```
        M M M M  ·  M M M M S
        M M M M  ·  M M M M
        P P·P P  ·  P P P P
        P P P P  ·  P P P P

  D        C              Ɑ

                  E

  D        L              Ɑ

        d d d d  ·  d d d d
        d d d d  ·  d d d d
        W W W W  ·  W W W W
       S W W W W  ·  W W W W
```

Front.

De Gomme's map shows Lord Byron's Regiment and the two divisions of Prince Rupert's Regiment, which formed a brigade under the command of Colonel Thomas Napier, deployed in advance of the main line of battle close to the ditch and in front of the innermost brigade of the right wing Horse. There is no immediately apparent reason why a brigade of Foot should be positioned in this exposed location where it masked the line of advance of part of the Horse.

It has been suggested that Napier's Brigade formed a 'night picket' to raise the alarm in the event of a night attack by the Allied army, but the musketeers lining the ditch were in a much better position to fulfil this role along the entire front of Rupert's army. The Parliamentarian pamphlet *A Full Relation ...* says that: 'There was a great Ditch between the Enemy and us, which ran along the front of the Battell, only between the Earl of Manchester's foot and the enemy there was a plain; in this Ditch the enemy had placed foure Brigades of their best Foot.'

Another suggestion is that Napier had been sent to defend the 'plain' at the point where the ditch levelled out. However, *A Full Relation ...* goes on to describe how the Scots brigades drove back the four Royalist brigades. The four brigades are therefore less likely to have been the three divisions of Napier's Brigade but rather part of the main Royalist first line.

Peter Newman has perhaps come closest to a credible explanation by suggesting that the Royalists had sited a battery of guns on a small hummock of firm ground in the area where Napier's Brigade stood. This is supported by accounts of the battle and it is likely that the Royalist artillerymen, finding their army arrayed on flat, soft moorland would have sought out any higher, firmer ground. Unfortunately Newman confuses the issue by his assumption that Napier's Brigade consisted entirely of musketeers, which is both tactically unlikely and unsupported by evidence.

The Imbattailing of many Squares in one Square.

Captaine.

Drum.		Drum.
sssss ppppp		sssss
sssss ppppp		sssss
sssss ppppp		sssss
sssss ppppp		sssss
sssss ppppp		sssss
ppppp		ppppp
ppppp		ppppp
ppppp	*Enſigne.*	ppppp
ppppp		ppppp
ppppp		ppppp
sssss ppppp		sssss
sssss ppppp		sssss
sssss ppppp		sssss
sssss ppppp		sssss
sssss ppppp		sssss

Lieutenant.

Here

Evidence for the presence of the Royalist guns comes from Lumsden in the letter written on 5 July that bore his sketch of the dispositions. He comments on the arrival of Rupert's army and on the start of the battle: 'We finding him so near and no possibility to have up our foot in two hours, keept the advantage of ane sleeke and the hills with our horss till the foot as they came up were put in order. In the meantyme we advanced our cannon and entred to play on them on the left wing, which maid them a littell to move; which they persaving brocht up thairs and gave us the lyk.'

Other sources mention that some of the Royalist Horse on the right wing suffered casualties from this artillery fire and were forced to withdraw. Lumsden makes clear that the Royalists brought up their own artillery to counter the Parliamentarian guns.

Daueutny Brimidgham

Prince Rupert's popularity as a Protestant hero worried the Parliamentarian propagandists and they quickly sought to portray him as the 'Bloody Prince' bringing the barbarism of the European wars to England.

Lieutenant-General Edmund Ludlow was not at Marston Moor, but he knew Cromwell and other participants. In his Memoirs he says that Prince Rupert:

'had gained an advantageous piece of ground upon Marston Moor, and caused a battery to be erected upon it, from which Capt. Walton, Cromwell's sister's son, was wounded by a shot in the knee. Whereupon Col. Cromwell commanded two field-pieces to be brought in order to annoy the enemy, appointing two regiments of foot to guard them ; who marching to that purpose, were attacked by the foot of the enemy's right wing, that fired thick upon them from the ditches. Upon this both parties seconding their foot, were wholly engaged, who before had stood only facing each other.'

Ludlow differs with Lumsden as to which side initiated the artillery duel, but crucially says 'both parties seconding their foot', which is to say brought up other units.

As a last question the deployment of Rupert's Foot as depicted on the de Gomme map is itself curious. If gaps on the right of the second line were left for Newcastle's Foot, the deployment of Rupert's divisions of Foot was inconsistent. Disregarding Newcastle's regiments the map shows 12 divisions in two lines, eight in the first and four in the second. During the 17th century Foot units did not draw up in lines with each unit standing next to one another. The normal deployment was that the front line drew up leaving gaps between each unit so that those in the second line positioned opposite the gap could if necessary march forward to fill the space and support the first line. Similarly the second line would leave gaps so that the first line could retire through them if it was defeated.

An army of 12 Foot divisions would probably draw up with seven divisions in the front line and five in the second corresponding to the five gaps in the first line. Rupert's dispositions are unbalanced as three divisions are missing from the right of the second line. We know that Napier's Brigade, consisting of three divisions, was posted to a location in front of the Horse. Was Napier's Brigade the missing three divisions?

Napier's Brigade was unusual because it contained Prince Rupert's Regiment of Foot, which as the commanding general's regiment was the senior Foot unit, and Lord Byron's Regiment of Foot, which as that of the commander of the cavalry of Rupert's army and overall second in command was the next most senior. Military protocol required that Rupert's regiment draw up on the right of the first line of the Foot. As part of Napier's Brigade, Byron's would be next in the front line. As confirmation it can be noted that third in command Sergeant-Major Tiller's Regiment was placed in the second-ranking post of honour on the left of the front line. As depicted on de Gomme's map the first line consists of experienced 'Irish' regiments except for Tyldesley's two divisions. The four units of the second line are made up of regiments that were newly raised or were collected by Rupert during his campaigning in Lancashire.

An explanation of the mysteries of Rupert's deployment may be found in the following course of events. Prince Rupert drew up his plan for a potential battle before he began his march on York in case he was forced to fight before he had united his army with that of Newcastle. His own regiment and Byron's stood on the right of the first line, which was composed of eight divisions, the others being experienced 'Irish' regiments. The second line was composed of the less experienced regiments except for Warren's 'Irish' veterans, who were on the right. Next to them were two divisions of Tyldesley's. This would provide a balanced deployment placing Rupert's most experienced eight divisions in the first

Rupert assisted the propaganda effort of his enemies by his ruthlessness in dealing with towns, such as Bolton, that resisted his assaults. 'The Cruelty of the Cavaliers' from a newspaper of 1644 goes beyond the reality of events.

line and his seven less experienced formations in the second line covering the gaps.

Arriving on Marston Moor, Rupert drew up his army in this formation in case he was attacked before the arrival of Newcastle's men. It would in any event be natural for his Foot to draw up in their pre-determined battle formation. The artillery duel begun, or responded to, by Cromwell developed into an infantry fire-fight with the result that Foot units needed to be hurried forward to protect the guns. Napier's Brigade standing on the right of the first line was the natural, and in effect, the only choice. As they marched away from their positions in the front line the three divisions of Tyldesley and Warren marched forward to take their places, leaving three spaces in the second line.

The battle around the guns may have brought on the general engagement and Napier's Brigade was unable to return to its position in the main line of Foot divisions as it was committed to protect the guns. Newcastle's seven divisions of Foot were directed to fill the three spaces on the right of Rupert's second line and the remaining four divisions

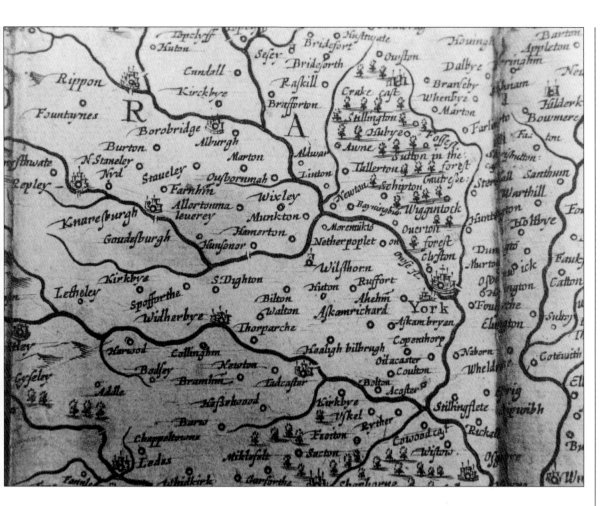

Hollar's map of 1644 marks 'Wilsthorn' and 'Bilton' but Long Marston and Tockwith do not rate a mention. Nether Poppleton is shown as 'Netherpoplet'. The extent of the Galtres Forest to the north of York where Rupert rested his army can be seen, as can the obstacles posed by the many substantial rivers in the area.

formed behind them making a third line covering the right rear of the Royalist infantry.

If this explanation is sound, de Gomme's map must show the Royalist dispositions as they were at, or shortly before, the start of the battle. De Gomme's ability to record, or with the help of participants, to reconstruct the Royalist dispositions is vindicated.

FIGHTING TACTICS

To understand the course of the battle of Marston Moor it is necessary to review tactical changes that had occurred during the first years of the Civil War.

Cavalry tactics

The most notable influence on Royalist tactical thinking was Prince Rupert, who combined high social standing with a keen interest in military science. Rupert was given a free hand in the matter of cavalry tactics as the King appointed him commander of the Horse of the Royal Army. His orders to his men were from the start a reflection of the Swedish tactics of Gustavus Adolphus that Rupert had studied during his captivity in Vienna. The Royalist Horse formed only three ranks deep

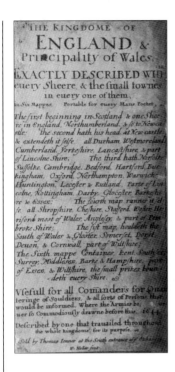

Hollar's set of folding maps of England are commended as 'Usefull for all Comanders for Quarteringe of Souldiers, & all sorts of persons that would be informed, Where the Armies be never so Commodiously drawne before this 1644'.

allowing them to overlap their opponents, who drew up in six ranks. Rupert was also determined that his men would meet the enemy at the charge. Sir Richard Bulstrode records that at Edgehill:

'Prince Rupert passed from one Wing to the other, giving positive Orders to the Horse, to march as close as possible, keeping their Ranks with Sword in hand, to receive the Enemy's Shot, without firing either Carbine or Pistol, till we broke in amongst the Enemy, and then to make use of our Fire-Arms as need should require.'

Rupert was fortunate that his scratch cavalry regiments were formed from the gentry and their servants, experienced horsemen in civilian life who held their 'rebel' opponents in contempt. A headlong charge once begun would carry his horsemen to contact with their enemy with no need for disciplined fire control or manoeuvring. Rupert was also fortunate to be present at the first significant cavalry skirmish at Powicke Bridge where his quick thinking and aggressive tactics took advantage of an unexpected meeting with a force of Parliamentarian Horse. The minor victory at Powicke Bridge raised the morale of the Royalist Horse to new heights and gave them an unquestioning confidence in their own superiority.

Had Rupert faced experienced troopers during these early encounters, or even an enemy employing the same tactics, the history of the Civil War might have been very different. The downfall of the Parliamentarian Horse was partly due to their adoption of tactics that, although sound, required well-trained and highly disciplined troopers to use effectively. The Parliamentarian Horse drew up six ranks deep and intended to receive the enemy at the halt, firing volleys of carbine and pistol shot to disrupt and halt the Royalist charge. Once Rupert's horsemen were halted and disorganised the Parliamentarians would charge forward in a body, making use of their swords and pistols to smash the confused mass of horsemen milling before them. In reality, their ragged volley of carbine and pistol shot failed to halt the Royalist charge at Edgehill and the inexperienced Parliamentarian troopers turned tail and ran. Rupert's Horse won their first major victory without needing to fight.

The morale ascendancy, superior tactics and the fear inspired by their commander's name made the Horse of the Royalist main armies invincible throughout the first year of the war. Parliament was slow to react to the string of defeats suffered by their Horse at the hands of Rupert and other Royalist commanders. The day to day need to raise, equip and train Horse to replace those lost in battle made it difficult to invest in new tactical methods and the necessary re-training of officers and men.

Some Parliamentarian commanders were more fortunate. After arriving towards the end of the battle of Edgehill, but in time to witness the superiority of the Royalist Horse, Oliver Cromwell returned to his native East Anglia to recruit and command the Horse of the Eastern Association of Parliamentarian counties. East Anglia offered advantages denied to most Parliamentarian commanders. Solidly Parliamentarian in its politics because of its Puritan religious beliefs, East Anglia was far away from Royalist-held areas. Recruiting and tax gathering could proceed unhindered and the troops of the Eastern Association were among the best equipped and trained of the civil wars. Cromwell was

Clifford's Tower was garrisoned during the siege of York as a lookout post for the defenders.

able to pick recruits of good character who shared his religious conviction that Parliament was fighting to save England in the name of God. Crucially he was able to pay his men regularly, which no doubt helped to reinforce their religious zeal.

Cromwell was quick to adopt tactics like those employed by Prince Rupert and he was fortunate to be able to give his troopers a baptism of fire in a number of small engagements against regional Royalist Horse on the borders of East Anglia. By the time of Marston Moor, Cromwell had been able to build a large force of well-trained and disciplined horsemen who had tasted victory and had complete faith in their officers, their comrades and in the righteousness of their cause.

The advantages afforded by his East Anglian base enabled Cromwell to make a thorough and highly effective change to his cavalry tactics, but other Parliamentarian armies and officers were making efforts in the same direction. Cromwell left no written account of his training, tactics or views on military matters. One officer who did set down his views was Captain John Vernon in a pamphlet called *The young Horse-man, or, The honest plain-dealing Cavalier* (*young* is used to mean inexperienced and *cavalier* refers to a mounted warrior rather than to a Royalist). Vernon's work was published in London at some time during 1644 and may have been written during the winter of 1643/44 while the armies were in quarters. The importance of Vernon's pamphlet is that it tells us how a junior officer of the Horse expected cavalry to fight in 1644. It is therefore a valuable description of the tactics used by the Parliamentarian Horse at Marston Moor. Vernon makes clear that three ranks is now the standard formation for the Parliamentarian Horse:

'All the Troops are to be drawn up into battalia, each being not above three deepe, likewise each troop must be at least a hundred paces distance

Newcastle's regiments probably marched out of York through Micklegate Bar on their way to join Prince Rupert at Marston Moor.

behind each other for the better avoiding of disorder, those troops that are to give the first charge being drawn up into battail as before, are to be at their close order, every left mans right knee must be close locked under his right hand mans left ham, as hath been shown before.'

The Parliamentarian Horse at Marston Moor was drawn up in this manner. Bernard de Gomme's map of the battle, although drawn from the Royalist perspective, shows the first two lines of the Parliamentarian army. Bodies of Horse are grouped into squadrons of one or two divisions, each made up of a number of troops. The second line is shown a good distance behind the first and the bodies are drawn up in a chequerboard formation so that the second line can move forward to fill gaps in the first line. Vernon continues by describing the manner of the charge. It is notable that he does not give any description of how to receive a charge, either at the halt or by counter charging and the inference is that Vernon expected Parliamentarian cavalry to take the initiative:

'In this order they are to advance toward the Enemy with an easy pace, firing their Carbines at a convenient distance, always aiming at their enemies brest or lower, because the powder is of an elevating nature, then drawing near the Enemy, they are with their right hands to take forth one of their pistols out of their houlsters, and holding the lock uppermost firing as before, always reserving one Pistol ready charged, spann'd and primed in your houlsters, in case of a retreat as I have shown before, having thus fired the troops are to charge the Enemy in full career, but in good order with their swords fastened with a Riband or the like unto their wrists, for fear of losing out of their hand, if they should chance to misse their blow, placing the pommel on their thigh, keeping still in their close order, locked as before.'

The advance toward the enemy was to be at an easy pace and when the pistols had been fired and the body had charged the enemy 'in full career', the close order and locked knee formation was to be retained. The final charge must have been of short duration or the body would have tended to break up. The emphasis was on striking as a tightly formed body aiming to push through the enemy body of Horse and smash its formation, so that only a disorganised mass of leaderless individual horsemen remained to be routed by the charge of supporting troops.

The cavalry fighting at Marston Moor saw the first major test of the new Parliamentarian cavalry tactics. On the left wing Cromwell's troopers rode forward in their locked bodies, that in which Cromwell rode himself consisting of 300 men. The second line moved forward in support, keeping a distance of 100 paces. The Royalists followed their standard tactics and moved forward in a counter-charge. Cromwell's first line was successful in partially disrupting the Royalist formation but the arrival of the Royalist second line held the Parliamentarian advance even when their supporting second line had been committed. Having spent their charges both sides had no alternative but to stand their ground and hack at their opponents, trying to retain their 'locked' formation while trying to break that of the enemy. The struggle was only decided by a flank attack by Scots Horse that broke the Royalist formation and threw them into disorder.

Against the Parliamentarian right wing the Royalist Horse did not employ their usual tactics but adapted to the ground before them. An unusual feature of the dispositions at Marston Moor was that all four

RIGHT **The Water Gate defended the city from attack from the west via the River Ouse.**

The Fisher Gate Postern Tower is now some distance from the river but during the siege its massive walls presented a daunting obstacle to any attack from the south of the city.

cavalry wings interspersed their bodies of Horse with groups of musketeers. This was a well-established tactic for a commander who expected to stand on the defensive and wished to add extra firepower to the defensive volleys of the carbines and pistols of his horsemen. The implication is that the commanders of all four cavalry wings expected to stand on the defensive that day; as soon as the cavalry advanced to the charge the supporting musketeers were left far behind.

Goring, the commander of the Royalist Horse on their left wing, faced Parliamentarian Horse advancing over rough ground crossed by hedges and ditches. He evidently considered that the disorganisation caused by these obstacles, and the casualties inflicted by the fire of his supporting musketeers, was sufficient to prevent the Parliamentarian Horse from charging home into his bodies of Horse and that he had no need to launch a counter-charge. In the event Goring was mistaken in the case of the 400 Horse formed up by Sir Thomas Fairfax who were able to defeat some units of his Horse. However, Fairfax's success was the exception and the confusion amongst the bulk of the Parliamentarian

37

Horse on this wing more than justified Goring's decision to keep his men in check. When their charge was finally made the Royalist Horse had little to do but drive the Parliamentarian Horse before them.

In victory a crucial difference emerged in the discipline of the rival cavalry. Goring's Royalists reacted to victory in the same way that they had to the defeat of the Parliamentarian Horse at Edgehill, the first major battle of the First Civil War, and in the same way that they would react in victory at Naseby, the last major battle of the First Civil War. The Royalist Horse set off in uncontrolled pursuit of their fleeing enemies and halted only to plunder their baggage train. By the time their commanders had recovered control and re-formed some into a fighting formation, the course of the battle they had left behind had turned against them.

In contrast Cromwell's men remained under the control of their officers and were quick to regain their formations so as to be ready to charge again. In Cromwell's own words: 'I raised such men as had the fear of God before them, and made some conscience of what they did.'

At Marston Moor both Rupert and Cromwell demonstrated that their cavalry was capable of defeating the enemy. Cromwell is remembered as the victor because he was able to hold his men together so that they could fight, and win, a second time.

Infantry tactics

Depending upon the number of men it could field, a regiment of Foot would draw up in one or two bodies or divisions, or in some cases be brigaded into a composite division. Each division would have a central body of pikemen with bodies of musketeers on the flanks.

Musketeers could also be posted without the support of pikemen to form a loose firing line. The so-called 'disbanded shot' tried to cause disruption in the ranks of an attacking enemy and to delay his formations by forcing his musketeers to be deployed to clear the way. At Marston Moor the Royalists positioned such a line of shot behind a ditch and hedge running across the battlefield but the suddenness of the Parliamentarian attack and a squall of rain deprived these musketeers of much of their effectiveness.

When attacked by cavalry the infantry body would draw up into a pike ring, an early equivalent of the square formation. The musketeers would crouch under the protection of the charged pike and attempt to keep up a fire sufficient to drive off the enemy Horse. Newcastle's Whitecoats probably adopted this tactic at the end of the battle, but found that the formation suffered when attacked by combined force of Horse, who prevented the pike ring from deploying, and musketeers or Dragoons who could pour shot into the huddled mass of defenders.

THE CAMPAIGN

Sir Henry Slingsby, who lived near Marston Moor and commanded one of the two Foot regiments that survived from the original garrison of York, wrote of the arrival of the Marquis of Newcastle's army in the city on 14 April 1644: 'His excellence his coming was diversely receiv'd; we in York were glad that we had ye assistance of his army, ye foot to be put into ye Citty for ye defence of it, ye horse to march to ye Prince to enable him the better to relieve us.'

The 'Prince' was Prince Rupert and Slingsby had good reason to expect that so famous a commander would come to the relief of York. Rupert had received nominal command in the North of England on 6 February, three days after the Scots arrived before the walls of Newcastle upon Tyne. With the Scots making little headway against the Northern Royalists there was no urgency for Rupert to go to their aid and others had greater need of his assistance. On 21 March Rupert, with a hastily assembled army, strong in cavalry, fell on the Parliamentarian forces of Sir John Meldrum who were besieging the vital Royalist town of Newark. Caught between the forces of Rupert and a sally by the Newark garrison of Sir Richard Byron, Sir John Meldrum was forced to surrender his entire army. Rupert's relief of Newark was one of the most notable and conclusive feats of arms of the Civil War and it may have been in Rupert's mind when he set about the similar operation of the relief of York. Rupert returned to Oxford and remained there between 25 April and 5 May.

To add to their defeats at Nantwich and Selby, on 29 March 1644 a Royalist army was decisively defeated at Cheriton. So little remained of the Southern army after this defeat that the surviving regiments were incorporated into the King's main Oxford army and the southern counties abandoned.

The new Royalist strategy was that the King would call in his garrisons and remain on the defensive with his Oxford army while Rupert raised an army from the recruiting grounds of Wales and Cheshire to relieve York. Rupert arrived in Lancashire with some 2,000 Horse and 6,000 Foot. An early cavalry clash at Garstang saw the rout of the Parliamentarians and panic spread throughout their local garrisons. Upon sight of the Royalist army the Parliamentarians at Stockport fled to the safety of the rudimentary defences of Bolton and on 28 May the town replied to Rupert's summons to surrender with cannon fire. The Royalist army swept into the town and butchered the garrison including many of the townspeople. According to the rules of war the garrison and population of a town that had refused a summons to surrender had forfeited the right to mercy. However the 'massacre at Bolton' became a staple of Parliamentarian propaganda and Rupert's demonized reputation as a black-hearted mercenary from the European wars was much reinforced.

On 30 May Rupert's army received a notable reinforcement when the cavalry of the Marquis of Newcastle's army joined it. Cavalry could do little to defend a besieged town and the demand for fodder to feed large numbers of horses made them a positive disadvantage to a garrison commander. Rupert now mustered a formidable force of some 7,000 Horse and 7,000 Foot.

THE RELIEF OF YORK

On 3 June the army of the Eastern Association under the command of the Earl of Manchester arrived to complete the encirclement of York. The garrison was in no immediate danger, but time was not on their side.

The threat to York was evident to King Charles for on 11 June he wrote to Rupert proposing that he march to the relief of the city. On 14 June the King sent another letter that again urged the relief of York. With what

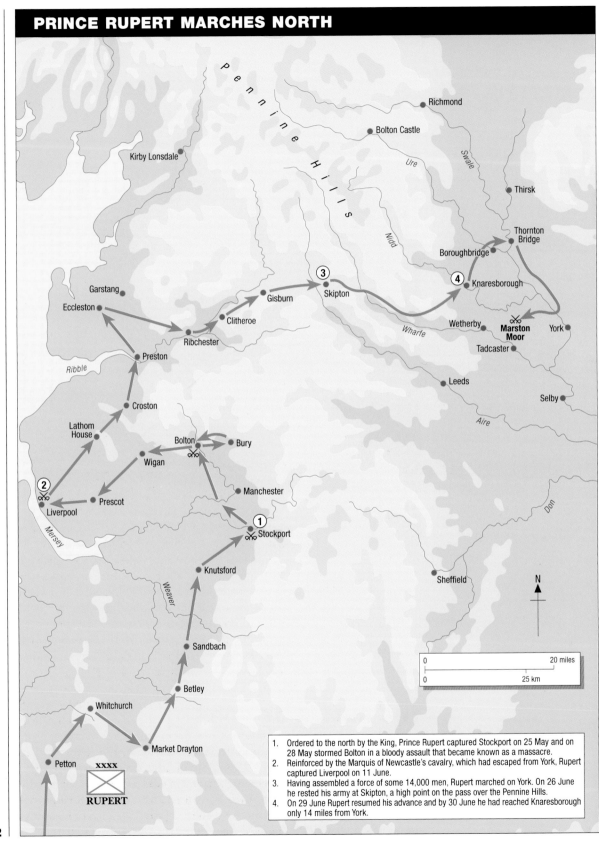

Pennine Hills

Richmond

Bolton Castle

Kirby Lonsdale

Ure

Swale

Thirsk

Thornton
Bridge

Boroughbridge

Nidd

4 Knaresborough

Garstang

Eccleston

Gisburn

3 Skipton

Clitheroe

Wetherby

Marston
Moor

York

Ribchester

Wharfe

Tadcaster

Preston

Ribble

Leeds

Croston

Selby

Lathom
House

Bolton

Bury

Aire

Wigan

Manchester

Petton

2 Liverpool

Prescot

Mersey

1 Stockport

Knutsford

Sheffield

N

Don

Weaver

Sandbach

0   20 miles

0   25 km

Betley

Whitchurch

XXXX

Market Drayton

RUPERT

1. Ordered to the north by the King, Prince Rupert captured Stockport on 25 May and on
    28 May stormed Bolton in a bloody assault that became known as a massacre.
2. Reinforced by the Marquis of Newcastle's cavalry, which had escaped from York, Rupert
    captured Liverpool on 11 June.
3. Having assembled a force of some 14,000 men, Rupert marched on York. On 26 June
    he rested his army at Skipton, a high point on the pass over the Pennine Hills.
4. On 29 June Rupert resumed his advance and by 30 June he had reached Knaresborough
    only 14 miles from York.

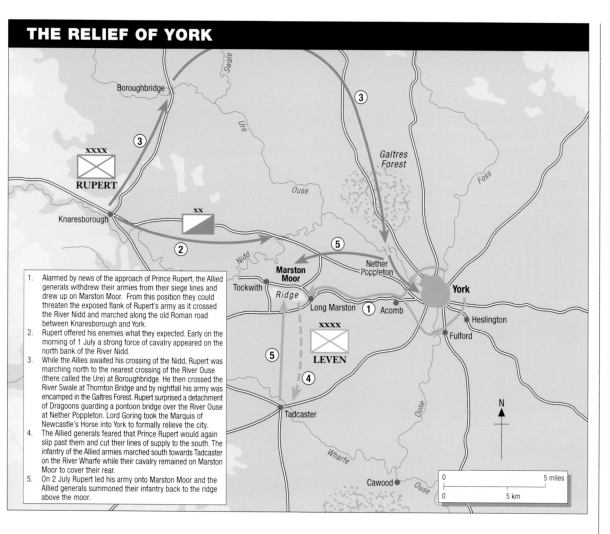

1. Alarmed by news of the approach of Prince Rupert, the Allied generals withdrew their armies from their siege lines and drew up on Marston Moor. From this position they could threaten the exposed flank of Rupert's army as it crossed the River Nidd and marched along the old Roman road between Knaresborough and York.
2. Rupert offered his enemies what they expected. Early on the morning of 1 July a strong force of cavalry appeared on the north bank of the River Nidd.
3. While the Allies awaited his crossing of the Nidd, Rupert was marching north to the nearest crossing of the River Ouse (there called the Ure) at Boroughbridge. He then crossed the River Swale at Thornton Bridge and by nightfall his army was encamped in the Galtres Forest. Rupert surprised a detachment of Dragoons guarding a pontoon bridge over the River Ouse at Nether Poppleton. Lord Goring took the Marquis of Newcastle's Horse into York to formally relieve the city.
4. The Allied generals feared that Prince Rupert would again slip past them and cut their lines of supply to the south. The infantry of the Allied armies marched south towards Tadcaster on the River Wharfe while their cavalry remained on Marston Moor to cover their rear.
5. On 2 July Rupert led his army onto Marston Moor and the Allied generals summoned their infantry back to the ridge above the moor.

degree of command or suggestion the letter directed Rupert toward confronting the enemy in battle is a matter on which historians still disagree. Rupert clearly thought that he had been ordered to repeat his feat of arms in the relief of Newark, for he carried the letter on his person for the rest of his life as evidence that his decision to fight at Marston Moor had been made in the light of direct orders from the King.

Rupert drew together the army that he had assembled in Lancashire and set off across the Pennine Hills for Yorkshire. By 26 June he was at Skipton Castle only 43 miles from York and here he paused for three days to rest his soldiers and to give warning of his approach to the York garrison.

The situation of Newcastle, locked up in York, was by no means desperate. He had occupied his opponents with treaty negotiations from 8 to 15 June. When, on 16 June, Major-General Crawford launched part of the Eastern Association army into an ill-coordinated attack presaged by the explosion of a mine under the walls of York, the Parliamentarians were beaten off losing 200 prisoners as well as heavy casualties. Lack of provisions was a more serious threat and Newcastle wrote urgently to Rupert seeking relief. On 28 June the Allied commanders outside York received messengers who told them that Rupert was approaching with 10,000 Horse and 8,000 Foot.

Between Monk Bar and Bootham Bar an indication of the original ditch that ran outside York city walls remains. Earth was piled against the walls inside and out to absorb the shock of cannon balls, which would shatter medieval masonry.

The Allied commanders determined to maintain the siege, to keep the garrison confined, while marching to intercept the relieving force. To achieve a successful encounter with Rupert and to blockade Newcastle's infantry in York they required more men. Sir John Meldrum's forces were recalled from Manchester and the Earl of Denbigh summoned with local forces from Staffordshire. Meldrum would arrive first, but not before 3 July.

News that Rupert's army was within a day's march of York threw these plans into confusion. With memories of the defeat outside Newark fresh in their minds the Allied generals hastily abandoned their siege lines containing their heavy guns and great store of ammunition and supplies, including 4,500 pairs of new shoes. Their objective now was to prevent Rupert adding the soldiers of the York garrison to his strength. Rupert's direct line of approach from Skipton should have brought him to York on the Knaresborough road. The Allied armies drew up on a ridge near the village of Long Marston, some five miles to the south-west of York. The Knaresborough road crossed in front of the ridge with the river Nidd at its back. Rupert could not march into York without facing the Allied armies as his flank would be exposed to attack and his line of retreat blocked by the Nidd. The York garrison could not march out to join Rupert at Knaresborough for the same reasons. The Allies' confidence in their position is demonstrated by an order sent out on the night of

29/30 June at Cromwell's command that 'My Lord Fairfax's troops that are in general parts of this country to march up either to us or to you, that they may not by their absence be made useless'. Once again the Allied generals had made their plans without reckoning on Rupert's skill as a commander.

Rupert's direct line of march to York was blocked. His army was substantially smaller than the 18,000 men with which the Allies credited him. A move to the south offered few prospects as the Allied armies could still intercept the Royalists before they had added the garrison of York to their strength. There remained an approach to York from the north, but this involved crossing the river Ouse that ran north-west from York, with the nearest crossing at Boroughbridge, which was farther from York than Knaresborough. The Allies had also found the river Ouse a problem when constructing their siege lines and they had built a bridge of boats at Poppleton, three miles to the north-west of York, to enable reinforcements to cross the Ouse in the event of a sally by the defenders. Should the Allies become aware of Rupert's attempt to reach York from the north they would have ample opportunity to pass their army over the Ouse by the bridge of boats at Poppleton to block his route while he made the long march north to Boroughbridge.

Early on the morning of 1 July, Royalist Horse advanced along the Knaresborough road to threaten the Allied armies at Long Marston. To the Allied generals this appeared to be the advance guard of Rupert's army, which as they expected was now moving to attempt the relief of York by giving them battle. The Allied armies hurriedly stood to arms and formed their brigades in accordance with their battle plans.

The day wore on and the main body of the Royalist army did not appear. No doubt this tardiness on Rupert's part came as a relief to the Allied generals for they could hope that the battle might yet be delayed until the reinforcements they were expecting had arrived. It was not until a detachment of Dragoons from the Eastern Association, who had been left to guard the bridge of boats at Poppleton, found themselves

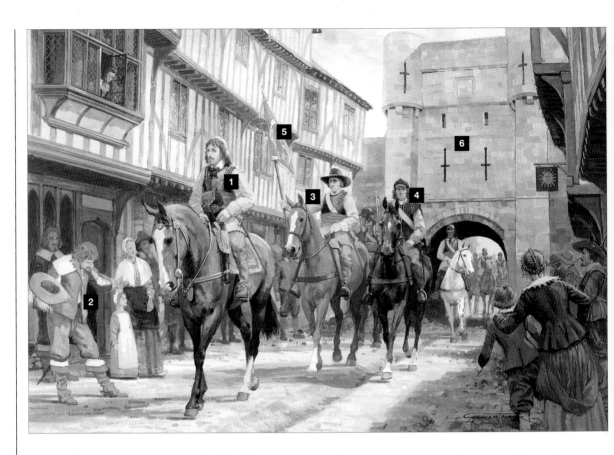

LORD GORING RELIEVES YORK AT THE HEAD OF NEWCASTLE'S HORSE (pages 46–47)

The bulk of the cavalry of Newcastle's army had been sent out of York to fight under Prince Rupert's command. Lord Goring (1), their General of Horse, joined them following his release as part of a prisoner of war exchange. It fell to Goring to enter York at the head of Newcastle's Horse as Rupert chose to remain with his army in their improvised encampment outside the city. Here Lord Goring is welcomed into the city by a gentleman of Newcastle's entourage (2). Behind Goring a Cornet of Horse (3) and a trumpeter (4) lead their troop into the city. The flag (5), known as a cornet like the junior officer who carries it, is based on one captured by the Parliamentarians at Marston Moor. It has a light green field and features a Cavalier cutting a complex knot with his sword. The motto 'This shall untie it' is a reference to Alexander the Great cutting the Gordian knot. Its meaning in this context is that, just as Alexander fulfilled the prophecy and conquered the Persian Empire, so the King is destined to conquer his enemies. The trumpeter is colourfully dressed reflecting his employment as a messenger and his non-combatant role. The gateways of the city, such as the towering Bootham Bar (6), had been packed with earth on the inside to prevent their wooden gates from being blown open with an explosive charge called a petard. The earth was intended to absorb the impact of the explosion and block the entrance to the attacking soldiers. Workmen were hurriedly employed to dig out the gates to allow Goring's troopers to enter the northern city gates while the western gates were also cleared to allow the horsemen and the garrison to march out the next day to join Prince Rupert's main army. The citizens of York gave their saviours a warm welcome as their arrival promised an end to the deprivations of life in a city under siege. All contact with the outside world had been severed once the Army of the Eastern Association arrived to complete the encirclement of the city in early June. However, trade and the opportunity for normal travel to other towns had been lost long before, when the Scots arrived outside the city in April. The influx of a several thousand of Newcastle's soldiers must have placed severe strain on the food supplies that were available to the ordinary townsfolk and soldiers often brought disease and contagion with them. Although York had been loyal to the King since he had fled to his northern capital in early 1642, long before hostilities had broken out, many of the townspeople must have seen the final surrender of their city after Marston Moor as a relief from misery and privation. (Graham Turner)

St Mary's Tower is a remarkable survival, not least because it was substantially rebuilt after being blown up by the mine exploded by the Eastern Association engineers in their abortive assault on the city on 16 June.

The countryside surrounding York in 1644 has long since been built over, but a few features remain. To the north of the University the much overgrown Mill Mound can still be seen. Allied artillery bombarded the city from this high ground.

brushed aside by the main body of the Royalist army that the Allied generals realised that they had been duped.

While part of his cavalry had put on a show to amuse the Allies at Long Marston, Rupert had marched the bulk of his army north to cross the Ouse at Boroughbridge, had then crossed its tributary the River Swale and marched south-east to seize the bridge of boats at Poppleton from the east bank of the Ouse. Rupert's army was now joined by his detached cavalry and reunited. York had been relieved without a shot fired.

The decision to fight

Five commanders of five independent armies now faced the same question. York had been relieved, what was to be done now? The position at Long Marston was no longer of importance to the Allied armies and each general thought of his lines of communication to his home base. The Fairfaxes and the Eastern Association army were well placed to fall back to Hull, the West Riding of Yorkshire and to East Anglia. The Scots were not so well placed with York blocking the direct road back to Scotland. Reinforcements from the town of Manchester and the county of Staffordshire were expected and a less exposed and more easily supplied location was needed so that the Allies could await their arrival and plan their next move. The town of Tadcaster, a few miles south of Long Marston, was selected as a useful road junction and plans were made for the Foot and baggage train to march there on 2 July, while the combined Horse of the three armies held the ridge above Long Marston to cover the rear of the marching columns.

The issues faced by the Royalist commanders proved more complex. The primary objective of Rupert's campaign had been achieved with the relief of York. Newcastle appears to have had no thought of pursuing the retreating Allied armies as his Foot regiments had endured the hardships of a long siege and he wished for a period of rest and

recruitment before undertaking further action. For Rupert other factors held sway as the relief of York had not been the sole objective of his campaign. The first day of July left several months of campaigning and Rupert did not intend to waste them. There may also have been the incentive that to equal his triumph before Newark he needed to destroy the enemy armies now retreating before him.

To add to these considerations was the letter that King Charles had written on 14 June when he had believed that his Oxford army was in danger of being caught between two pursuing Parliamentarian armies. After discussing the supply of gun powder the letter said:

> *But now I must give you the true state of my affairs, which if their condition be such as enforces me to give you more peremptory commands than I would willingly do, you must not take it ill. If York be lost I shall esteem my crown little less; unless supported by your sudden march to me; and a miraculous conquest in the South, before the effects of their Northern power can be found here. But if York be relieved, and you beat the rebels army of both kingdoms, which are before it; then (but otherwise not) I may make a shift (upon the defensive) to spin out time until you come to assist me. Wherefore I command and conjure you, by the duty and affection which I know you bear me, that all new enterprises laid aside, you immediately march, according to your first intention, with all your force to the relief of York. But if that be either lost, or have freed themselves from the besiegers, or that from want of powder, you cannot undertake that work, that you immediately march with your whole strength to Worcester, to assist me and my army; without which, or you having relieved York by beating the Scots, all the successes you can afterwards have must infallibly be useless unto me. You may believe that nothing but an extreme necessity could make me write thus unto you, wherefor, in this case, I can no ways doubt of your punctual compliance with*
> *Your loving uncle and faithful friend*
> *CHARLES R.*
> *P.S. – I command this Bearer to speak to you concerning Vavasour Ticknell June 14th 1644*

Historians have disagreed over what the King intended this letter to convey to Rupert. Peter Newman has written: 'The letter is less a letter of instruction than one of information, news and advice, confirming that what Rupert had marched north to achieve was still, in the King's opinion, worth attempting.' Peter Young pointed out that a modern staff officer would find it hard to see in the letter a direct order to fight a battle after York had been relieved. However, Young acknowledged that the King and his council knew Rupert, were familiar with his temperament and must have expected him to fight if he had the chance.

Stuart Reid has risen to Rupert's defence and has drawn attention to the fact that in the letter the King specifically explained why his commands were more peremptory than he would have wished, and that the final sentence stresses the King's 'extreme necessity' and demands 'punctual compliance'.

Perhaps the clearest interpretation of the letter comes from a contemporary, Lord Culpeper, who arrived after its dispatch. On hearing that the letter had been sent on its way, Culpeper declared: 'Why then,

St Lawrence's Church was stormed by the Scots and used as a gun position to bombard the city. A Victorian church stands on the site but the original tower remains.

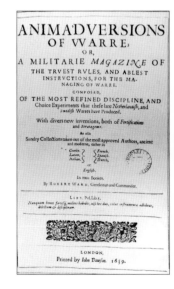

Robert Ward's *Animadversions of Warre*, published in London in 1639, contained extensive advice on the means to be employed in attacking and defending towns.

In 1642 there were few places in England that could claim to have modern fortifications. Several cities, such as York, retained their medieval walls and Robert Ward offered advice on how to make the best of what was available to the defenders.

before God you are undone, for upon this peremptory order he will fight, whatever comes on't!'

The truth may be that the letter was written at a time when the King and his Council believed themselves to be in danger of imminent defeat by the Parliamentarian armies that were pursuing them. Once this threat had receded and Rupert had lost the battle for the North, the panic-ridden message became an embarrassment and its rambling nature was used to obscure the meaning of the direct commands it contained.

What can be stated with certainty is that Rupert believed that he had been ordered to defeat the Scots and their Allies in addition to relieving York and to do so with all speed.

At about midday on 1 July, Major William Legge arrived at Newcastle's lodgings with fresh orders. Rupert intended to give battle the following day and wished Newcastle's army to march out to Marston Moor to join his forces that were assembling there. At first Newcastle agreed to meet the Prince with all his forces and Rupert duly roused his army early on 2 July and set it to march to the moor. Newcastle was requested to have his regiments on the moor by 4.00am.

Newcastle and his senior military advisor, General King, who had been ennobled as Lord Eythin, did not wish to seek battle and it has been suggested that they deliberately held their regiments back. In fact on the afternoon of 1 July the York garrison had discovered that the Allied siege lines were empty of soldiers but full of abandoned supplies and they had set out to loot to their hearts' content.

Newcastle's cavalry, which had served under Rupert since their escape to Lancashire, had entered York to return to their own army. On 2 July they did not march out to Marston Moor until 9.00am which, given the short distance involved, indicates that they had not been mustered with any haste. Of the infantry regiments there remained no sign.

Newcastle, with his troop of 'gentlemen of quality', joined Prince Rupert at around 9.00am to be greeted with the welcome 'My Lord, I wish you had come sooner with your forces, but I hope we shall yet have a glorious day.' This was the first meeting between the commanders of

One option was to construct earth forts outside the old defences to try to keep the artillery of the besiegers away from the walls. Such a fort was constructed on rising ground to the west of York, but it fell to a storming party from the Scots army.

Ward also offered advice to besiegers on the usefulness of pontoon bridges that could be carried in the baggage train of a marching army so as to be ready for immediate use.

the two Royalist armies, as Rupert had chosen to stay with his army despite Newcastle's invitation to enter York 'to consult'.

In her biography Newcastle's wife reported that the Marquis 'declared his mind to the Prince, desiring his Highness not to attempt anything as yet upon the enemy; for he had intelligence that there was some discontent between them, and that they were resolved to divide themselves, and so to raise the siege without fighting.' Prince Rupert replied that 'he had a letter from his Majesty … with a positive and absolute command to fight the enemy'. Newcastle had no option but to give way, although Rupert did not show him the letter and he therefore had no opportunity to make his own evaluation of what it might in fact require of the Prince.

There was good reason to think that the Allied armies might soon part company. Counting non-combatants and camp followers, their host cannot have numbered less than 30,000 mouths to feed with perhaps as many horses requiring daily fodder. Soon each commander would have to look to his own lines of supply. Tadcaster had been a suitable compromise for an interim rendezvous, but the next marches would take the Allied armies in different directions. The Earl of Manchester would fall back southward to Lincoln to cover the Eastern Association counties. The Fairfaxes would have to consider the needs of Hull to the east and the Parliamentarian towns of the West Riding to the west. Exactly where the Scots could hope for welcome and supply was probably not clear to the Earl of Leven. Home was to the north, but so was the Royalist army.

It could be hoped that given time the Allied armies might disperse to the four points of the compass, but time was something that the King's letter did not allow Prince Rupert. His exchange with Newcastle provides evidence of the way the King's letter had come to dominate Rupert's appreciation of the strategic situation facing the Royalist cause. Rupert believed that the King and the Oxford army faced imminent defeat and that his duty as detailed in the letter was to relieve York, defeat the Scots and Parliamentarian armies, and then to hurry south with all haste to save the King and the kingdom.

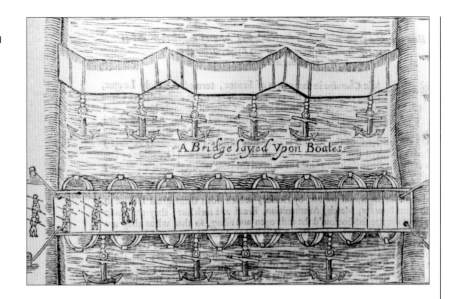

Sources differ as to whether the meeting between Rupert and Newcastle took place on the battlefield or on the line of march from York. Regardless, by the time of their meeting, events had begun to change the tactical position and the opportunity for an early Royalist attack had faded.

The Allied army was mustered early on 2 July with the intent of completing the march to Tadcaster in good time. Simeon Ash, the Earl of Manchester's chaplain, writing from York on 10 July 1644, recorded: 'Upon tuesday morning, a partie of the enemies horse, having faced us awhile, wheeled back out of sight, which gave us cause to suspect that a maine body was marched towards Tadcaster (having relived Yorke), where he might cut off the river, and so both scant us of provisions and get down suddainly into the South. Hereupon our foot, with Artillery, were commanded to advance towards Tadcaster. The Scots (marching in the Van that day) being got almost to Tadcaster, and the Earl of Manchester's foot being two or three miles from Marston, we had a very hot alarum that the enemy with all his strength was returned to the Moore.'

Had Rupert been able to mount an attack in strength while the Allied foot and cannon were retracing their steps to the moor or while they were in the confusion of re-forming their line of battle, he must have achieved an advantage that would have thrown his enemies into disarray.

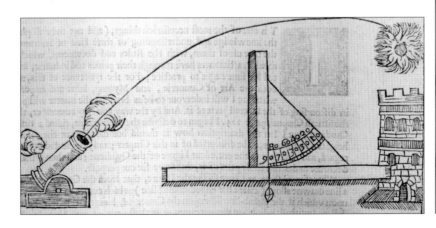

The cavalry of the Allied armies retired to draw up in battle formation on the ridge overlooking Marston Moor. From this position they were able to cover the rear of their infantry and baggage on the march. As matters stood, Rupert was forced to wait while Allied Foot regiments reached the ridge above the moor and formed into line, and still Newcastle's infantry did not come. Ash reports that by 2.00–3.00pm the Allied army had re-formed. The soldiers trampled down the rye crop growing on the ridge and shivered as unseasonable showers of rain fell from time to time.

Terrain

Marston Moor is 49ft, and the ridge up to 141ft, above sea level. The highest point, known as 'Cromwell's Plump' after a group of trees that grows there, offered the Parliamentarian commanders a panoramic view over Prince Rupert's dispositions and far away to the walls of York.

The ground falls steeply from the high points of the ridge but runs down to the beginning of the moor proper as a gentle slope. Hidden from the view of an observer on the moor, and not clearly depicted by the 5m (16ft) spaced contours of the modern Ordnance Survey map, is 'the Glen'. The slope of the ridge falls into a narrow valley before rising up again and then continuing its gradual descent to the moor. The ridge is in fact a double ridge with an area of dead ground in which, in the dark of night at the end of the battle, several hundred disorganised Royalist cavalry sheltered before slipping away to York unnoticed by the Allies.

At the time of the battle the ridge was under cultivation with a mixture of rye and wheat. Sir Thomas Fairfax recorded that the ground where the Horse of the Allied right wing drew up was broken by undergrowth and his line of advance blocked by hedges and ditches. On the Allied left wing, the area known as Bilton Bream required the services of pioneers to level hedges and a man-made rabbit warren, to make it fit for cavalry to manoeuvre.

To the front of the ridge a track ran east to west connecting the villages of Long Marston and Tockwith. Beyond the track a hedged drainage ditch formed a boundary between the cultivated higher ground and the moor.

On the moor itself Wilstrop Wood formed a dominant feature to the north. Some cultivated land did exist on the fringes of the moor, such as the 'bean land' where Prince Rupert is alleged to have hidden. Animals grazed on the moor. Areas such as 'White Syke Close' may have had ditches or hedges to help pen the flocks.

As its name indicates Long Marston was a straggling village and it formed the eastern boundary of the battlefield. To the west the village of Tockwith was a limit to the battle lines. There is no indication in any account that any fighting took place in either village or that either side attempted to form strongpoints in the houses of the villages.

THE BATTLE

At about 9.00am the Royalist cavalry appeared on the edge of the moor. The Allied Horse withdrew up to the top of the ridge into the cornfields which covered the fertile higher ground. The Royalists recognised the defensive value of the ridge and attempted to establish a foothold on the western end of the ridge at an area called Bilton Bream. The Parliamentarian author of the narrative *A Full relation ...* carried to London by Captain Stewart related: 'In the meanwhile the Enemy perceiving that our Cavalry had possessed themselves of a cornhill, and having discovered neer unto that hill a place of great advantage, where they might have both Sun and Winde of us, advanced thither with a Regiment of Red Coats and a party of Horse; but we understanding well their intentions, and how prejudiciall it would be unto us if they should keep that ground, we sent out a party which beat them off, and planted there our left wing of Horse.'

The Allied left wing was made up of the cavalry of the Eastern Association under Cromwell's command. The skirmish was an important victory as the dispositions of the main armies were now established, with the Allies in possession of the full length of the ridge and the Royalists confined to the moorland below.

A salvo of cannon fire, a mere four shots, followed from the Allied position, but as Sir Henry Slingsby recorded: 'This was only a shewing their teeth, for after 4 shots made them give over, & in Marston Corn fields falls to singing psalms.'

At some time between 2.00pm and 4.00pm, Newcastle's Foot regiments began to arrive on the battlefield with their commander, General King. A number of none too friendly exchanges are recorded as having taken place between the Royalist commanders. 'The Prince demanded of [General] King how he liked the marshalling of his army, who replied he did not approve of it being drawn too near the enemy, and in place of disadvantage, then said the Prince, "they may be drawn to a further distance". " No sir" said King "it is too late."'

This exchange was recorded by the Governor of Scarborough where Newcastle and General King took ship for Europe after the battle was lost. It may be that hindsight assisted in the recollection of the advice offered, of how boldly it was given and how meekly it was answered. Given the events of the battle it seems unlikely that Prince Rupert would have been unaware of the strength of his defensive position. The suggestion that he would so readily have offered to abandon those defences in response to King's off-hand criticism seems highly unlikely given the circumstances and the character of the Prince.

The contemporary historian the Earl of Clarendon recorded: 'When Major-General King came up Prince Rupert showed the Marquis and the Earle a paper, which he said was the draught of the battle as he meant to fight it, and asked them what they thought of it. King answered, "By God, Sir, it is very fine in the paper, but there is no such thing in the field." The Prince replied, "Not so," etc. The Marquis asked the Prince what he would do? His Highness answered, "We will charge them tomorrow morning." My Lord asked him, whether he were sure the enemy would not fall on them sooner; he answered No; and the Marquis goes to his coach hard by, and calling for a pipe of tobacco, before he could take it the enemy charged.'

Once again the foresight attributed to Newcastle is inconsistent with his military reputation. The Duchess of Newcastle's memoir asserts that the Prince told her husband that there would be no action that day. This may only serve to confirm that Newcastle or one of his staff was the source of Clarendon's account.

Whatever their conversation, it is certain that the Royalist commanders, like their common soldiers, were taken by surprise when the Allied line began to move forward down from the ridge. The troopers of Horse had dismounted and the pikemen and musketeers were sitting in rank and file taking their ease and preparing what food they had brought with them. Newcastle was in his coach and Rupert was dismounted and unprepared for action.

Contemporary accounts do not make it clear how the Allied armies came to launch their attack in the evening of 2 July. It has been suggested that the fact that the Royalist army was standing down, and that cooking fires had been lit, caused the Earl of Leven to seize his opportunity with his enemies at a disadvantage.

An alternative explanation is that an artillery duel had developed between Royalist guns, placed on an area of high ground in front of their right wing Horse, and Parliamentarian guns that had caused casualties amongst Byron's Horse forcing them to withdraw. Suffering casualties in return, including his nephew, Cromwell ordered his guns forward with two infantry regiments in support. The Royalists countered by deploying Prince Rupert's and Lord Byron's Regiments of Foot from out of their front line and a brisk fire-fight developed. The Allied armies were drawn into an attack all along their line as the Royalists fell back.

At York the besiegers resorted to tunnelling towards the city walls. This involved accurate surveying to ensure that the tunnellers kept digging in the right direction and stopped when under their target.

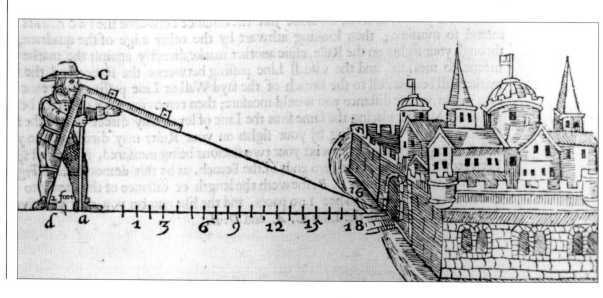

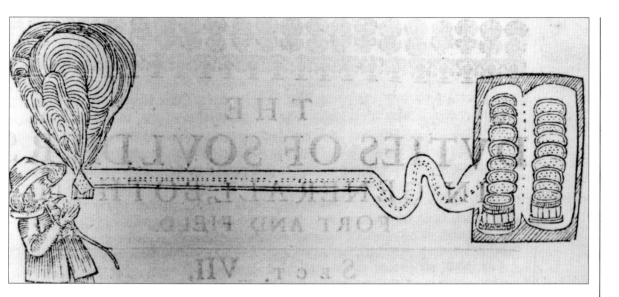

The Allied pikemen and musketeers broke into a 'running march' taking advantage of the slope that they were descending. The Royalist skirmishers defending the hedge and ditch were thrown into confusion by the unexpected attack and only a proportion had the match cord with which they fired their muskets ready lit. They were not helped by a sudden burst of thunder and rain that swept over the battlefield.

On the left of the Allied infantry the brigades of the Eastern Association under Major-General Crawford outflanked the Foot regiments of Prince Rupert and Lord Byron which had been stationed to defend the guns and these fell back towards the main Royalist line. In the centre of the Allied Foot the Brigade of Lord Fairfax broke through the hedge and pushed back the defending Royalist regiments. The Allied infantry swept over the ditch capturing four small cannons of the class called 'drakes', which had been positioned to support the Royalist skirmishers. On the right of the Allied Foot, the Scots Brigades made less progress, largely due to the disaster that was overtaking the Allied right wing Horse.

Engineers from Manchester's Army dug under St Mary's Tower to the north-west of York. Their mine was in danger of flooding and it was exploded prematurely. The tower was destroyed and the defences breached but supporting attacks by the other armies were not ready and the assault was beaten back with heavy losses. Note the 'S' bend in the tunnel which prevents the force of the blast from travelling back up the tunnel, directing it instead against the defences under siege.

THE DEFEAT OF FAIRFAX'S HORSE

Sir Thomas Fairfax commanded on the Allied right wing. Like the Royalists facing him, Fairfax had drawn up his Horse with bodies of musketeers interspersed between his squadrons. This was a defensive formation, having the intention that the fire of the musketeers would break up a body of attacking Horse. Fairfax recorded his problems with the right wing in *A short Memorial of the Northern Actions: during the War there, from the year 1642 till the year 1644*: 'Our Right Wing had not, all, so good success, by reason of the whins and ditches which we were to pass over before we could get to the Enemy, which put us into great disorder: notwithstanding, I drew up a body of 400 Horse. But because the intervals of Horse, in this Wing [of the Royalist horse] only, were lined with Musketeers; which did us much hurt with their shot.'

Fairfax with his 400 men broke the enemy Horse opposed to them and pursued them towards York. In his absence, the advance of the main force

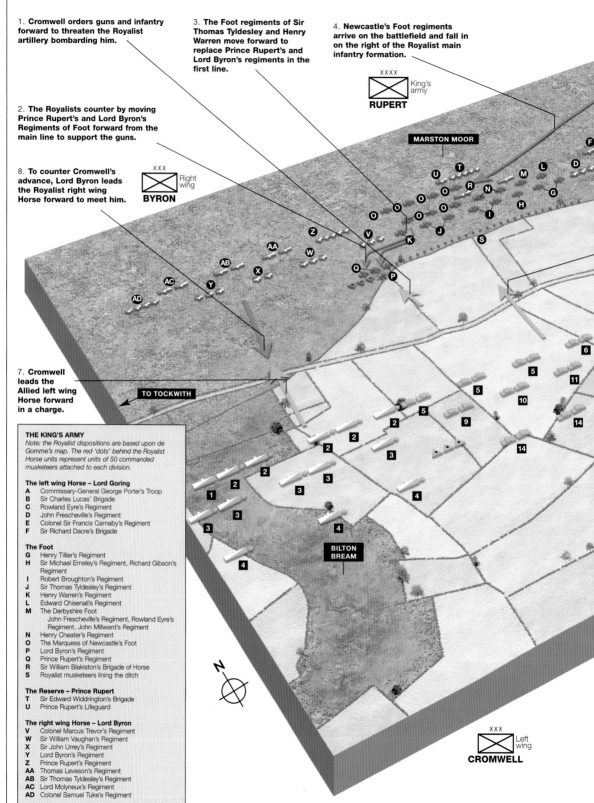

1. **Cromwell orders guns and infantry forward to threaten the Royalist artillery bombarding him.**

3. **The Foot regiments of Sir Thomas Tyldesley and Henry Warren move forward to replace Prince Rupert's and Lord Byron's regiments in the first line.**

4. **Newcastle's Foot regiments arrive on the battlefield and fall in on the right of the Royalist main infantry formation.**

2. **The Royalists counter by moving Prince Rupert's and Lord Byron's Regiments of Foot forward from the main line to support the guns.**

8. **To counter Cromwell's advance, Lord Byron leads the Royalist right wing Horse forward to meet him.**

7. **Cromwell leads the Allied left wing Horse forward in a charge.**

XXXX
King's army
RUPERT

MARSTON MOOR

XXX
Right wing
BYRON

TO TOCKWITH

BILTON BREAM

XXX
Left wing
CROMWELL

N

THE KING'S ARMY
Note: the Royalist dispositions are based upon de Gomme's map. The red 'dots' behind the Royalist Horse units represent units of 50 commanded musketeers attached to each division.

The left wing Horse – Lord Goring
A   Commissary-General George Porter's Troop
B   Sir Charles Lucas' Brigade
C   Rowland Eyre's Regiment
D   John Frescheville's Regiment
E   Colonel Sir Francis Carnaby's Regiment
F   Sir Richard Dacre's Brigade

The Foot
G   Henry Tillier's Regiment
H   Sir Michael Erneley's Regiment, Richard Gibson's Regiment
I   Robert Broughton's Regiment
J   Sir Thomas Tyldesley's Regiment
K   Henry Warren's Regiment
L   Edward Chisenall's Regiment
M   The Derbyshire Foot
        John Frescheville's Regiment, Rowland Eyre's Regiment, John Millward's Regiment
N   Henry Cheater's Regiment
O   The Marquess of Newcastle's Foot
P   Lord Byron's Regiment
Q   Prince Rupert's Regiment
R   Sir William Blakiston's Brigade of Horse
S   Royalist musketeers lining the ditch

The Reserve – Prince Rupert
T   Sir Edward Widdrington's Brigade
U   Prince Rupert's Lifeguard

The right wing Horse – Lord Byron
V   Colonel Marcus Trevor's Regiment
W   Sir William Vaughan's Regiment
X   Sir John Urrey's Regiment
Y   Lord Byron's Regiment
Z   Prince Rupert's Regiment
AA   Thomas Leveson's Regiment
AB   Sir Thomas Tyldesley's Regiment
AC   Lord Molyneux's Regiment
AD   Colonel Samuel Tuke's Regiment

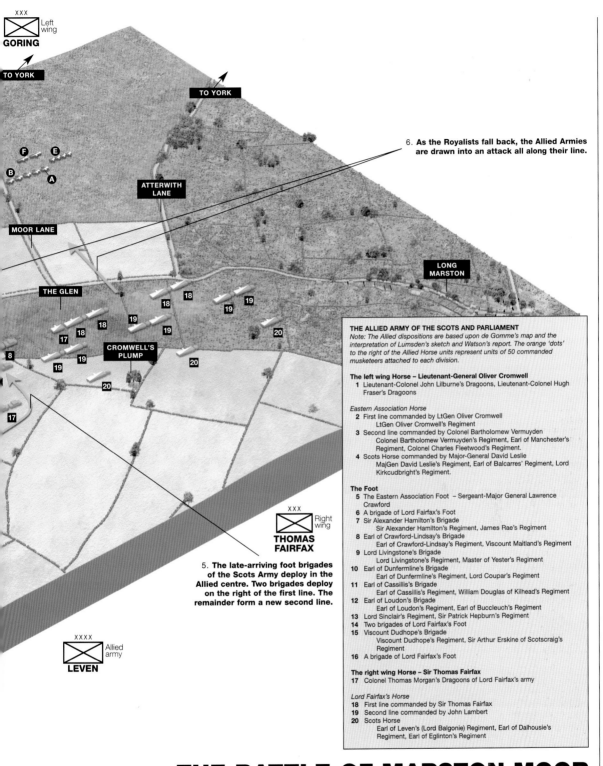

XXX
Left wing
GORING

← TO YORK

↗ TO YORK

6. As the Royalists fall back, the Allied Armies are drawn into an attack all along their line.

F E
B A

ATTERWITH LANE

MOOR LANE

LONG MARSTON

THE GLEN

18 18 19
19 19
17 18 18 19
17 19
8 19
19
20
20 20

CROMWELL'S PLUMP

17

XXX
Right wing
THOMAS FAIRFAX

5. The late-arriving foot brigades of the Scots Army deploy in the Allied centre. Two brigades deploy on the right of the first line. The remainder form a new second line.

XXXX
Allied army
LEVEN

THE ALLIED ARMY OF THE SCOTS AND PARLIAMENT
Note: The Allied dispositions are based upon de Gomme's map and the interpretation of Lumsden's sketch and Watson's report. The orange 'dots' to the right of the Allied Horse units represent units of 50 commanded musketeers attached to each division.

The left wing Horse – Lieutenant-General Oliver Cromwell
1 Lieutenant-Colonel John Lilburne's Dragoons, Lieutenant-Colonel Hugh Fraser's Dragoons

Eastern Association Horse
2 First line commanded by LtGen Oliver Cromwell
      LtGen Oliver Cromwell's Regiment
3 Second line commanded by Colonel Bartholomew Vermuyden
      Colonel Bartholomew Vermuyden's Regiment, Earl of Manchester's Regiment, Colonel Charles Fleetwood's Regiment.
4 Scots Horse commanded by Major-General David Leslie
      MajGen David Leslie's Regiment, Earl of Balcarres' Regiment, Lord Kirkcudbright's Regiment.

The Foot
5 The Eastern Association Foot – Sergeant-Major General Lawrence Crawford
6 A brigade of Lord Fairfax's Foot
7 Sir Alexander Hamilton's Brigade
      Sir Alexander Hamilton's Regiment, James Rae's Regiment
8 Earl of Crawford-Lindsay's Brigade
      Earl of Crawford-Lindsay's Regiment, Viscount Maitland's Regiment
9 Lord Livingstone's Brigade
      Lord Livingstone's Regiment, Master of Yester's Regiment
10 Earl of Dunfermline's Brigade
      Earl of Dunfermline's Regiment, Lord Coupar's Regiment
11 Earl of Cassillis's Brigade
      Earl of Cassillis's Regiment, William Douglas of Kilhead's Regiment
12 Earl of Loudon's Brigade
      Earl of Loudon's Regiment, Earl of Buccleuch's Regiment
13 Lord Sinclair's Regiment, Sir Patrick Hepburn's Regiment
14 Two brigades of Lord Fairfax's Foot
15 Viscount Dudhope's Brigade
      Viscount Dudhope's Regiment, Sir Arthur Erskine of Scotscraig's Regiment
16 A brigade of Lord Fairfax's Foot

The right wing Horse – Sir Thomas Fairfax
17 Colonel Thomas Morgan's Dragoons of Lord Fairfax's army

Lord Fairfax's Horse
18 First line commanded by Sir Thomas Fairfax
19 Second line commanded by John Lambert
20 Scots Horse
      Earl of Leven's (Lord Balgonie) Regiment, Earl of Dalhousie's Regiment, Earl of Eglinton's Regiment

THE BATTLE OF MARSTON MOOR

2 July 1644, viewed from the south-west. Early evening. Prince Rupert spends the day awaiting the arrival of Newcastle's Foot regiments on the moor. As they form up with his army the Prince decides it is too late to attack that day and orders his men to fall out from their ranks to rest and eat. At this point the Allied Armies surge down from the ridge in a general assault.

When the Royalist garrison of York explored the Allied siege lines that had been abandoned at the news of Rupert's approach, they found a great deal to plunder. This illustration shows the kind of formal camp that a besieging general was advised to construct to keep his men healthy.

of Allied Horse collapsed into confusion amongst the whins (hedges and bracken) and the ditches that covered the area. As they emerged onto the moor they faced a steep embankment running down to the level ground. Under fire from Royalist musketeers they suffered heavy casualties and were unable to form up to meet the charge of the Royalist Horse which swept them from the battlefield. The rout continued back over the ridge until the Royalists were lured away by the greater attraction of the plunder offered by the Allied baggage train. Fairfax appears to have been unable to prevent his small force of victorious horsemen from pursuing their defeated enemy from the field as he returned alone, and was obliged to remove the field sign which showed him to be of the Allied army. He was able to make his way to the Eastern Association Horse by passing unrecognised through part of the victorious Royalist army.

THE CLASH OF CROMWELL'S AND RUPERT'S HORSE

On the Allied left wing Cromwell led his cavalry forward. Like Sir Thomas Fairfax, he had positioned himself with the front line squadrons amongst a division of 300 troopers from his own regiment. Like Fairfax, Cromwell's enthusiasm to be in the thick of the fighting was to be at the cost of a wound and a temporary loss of control of his command.

Lord Byron, commander of the Royalist right wing cavalry opposed to Cromwell, had not taken advantage of the chance to leave his post to partake of a meal or a pipe as had Rupert and Newcastle. Byron has received much of the blame for the defeat at Marston Moor for his haste in counter-charging Cromwell. It is only fair to note that Byron was at his post and that his command was able to react almost immediately to the surprise of the attack upon them.

Byron is accused of throwing away the advantages of the strong defensive position devised for him by Rupert, by making an ill-considered charge across obstacles that he should have defended. The notes contained in *Prince Rupert's Diary* state that while awaiting Newcastle's forces Rupert: 'drew his forces into a Strong posture making his Post as strong as possibly he could ...

Ld Biron then made a Charge upon Cromwell's forces.

Represent here ye Posture the P[rince] put ye forces in and how by ye improper charge of ye Ld Byron much harm was done.'

The *Life of James II* says of Byron: 'Prince Rupert had posted him very advantageously behind a warren and a slough, with a positive command not to quit his ground, but in that posture only to expect and receive the charge of the enemy.'

Both these accounts date from the period of the exile of Charles II and his Restoration and are based upon the recollections of many years previously.

Stuart Reid has come to Byron's defence and has argued that as Rupert was not expecting the Allies to advance that day, he is unlikely to have given detailed instructions for the conduct of the right wing Horse if attacked. Reid points out that at this part of the line of battle the ditch was not a serious obstacle, forming no more than an area of muddy standing water. Byron was likely to have a better understanding of the

The line of Moor Lane can still be traced running from beside the monument towards the Royalist positions.

defensive value of the ground in front of him than other commanders or observers. Reid interprets the Parliamentarian Scoutmaster Watson's account as confirming that Cromwell's Horse had cleared the ditch before they encountered Byron's attack. However, when Watson writes of passing the ditch and 'going in a running march' he is clearly describing the advance of the Foot at this point:

'All the Earle of Manchesters Foot being three Brigades, began the charge with their bodies against the Earls of Newcastle, and Prince Ruperts bravest Foot. In a moment we were passed the ditch into the Moore, upon equall grounds with the enemy, our men going in a running march. Our front divisions of horse charged their front, Lieutenant Generall Cromwels division of three hundred Horse, in which himselfe was in person, charged the first division of Prince Ruperts …'

Byron does seem to have forfeited the support of the bodies of musketeers which were interspersed with his squadrons and which were to prove so destructive of Sir Thomas Fairfax's Horse on the Royalist left wing, although that destruction was probably the greater given that Fairfax's Horse was caught immobile and disorganised after emerging

61

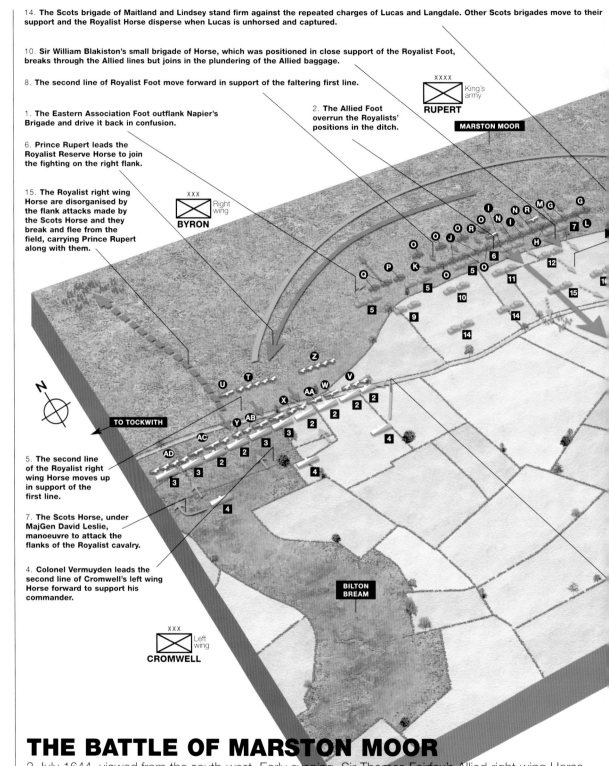

14. The Scots brigade of Maitland and Lindsey stand firm against the repeated charges of Lucas and Langdale. Other Scots brigades move to their support and the Royalist Horse disperse when Lucas is unhorsed and captured.

10. Sir William Blakiston's small brigade of Horse, which was positioned in close support of the Royalist Foot, breaks through the Allied lines but joins in the plundering of the Allied baggage.

8. The second line of Royalist Foot move forward in support of the faltering first line.

1. The Eastern Association Foot outflank Napier's Brigade and drive it back in confusion.

2. The Allied Foot overrun the Royalists' positions in the ditch.

6. Prince Rupert leads the Royalist Reserve Horse to join the fighting on the right flank.

15. The Royalist right wing Horse are disorganised by the flank attacks made by the Scots Horse and they break and flee from the field, carrying Prince Rupert along with them.

5. The second line of the Royalist right wing Horse moves up in support of the first line.

7. The Scots Horse, under MajGen David Leslie, manoeuvre to attack the flanks of the Royalist cavalry.

4. Colonel Vermuyden leads the second line of Cromwell's left wing Horse forward to support his commander.

XXXX — King's army
RUPERT

MARSTON MOOR

XXX — Right wing
BYRON

TO TOCKWITH

BILTON BREAM

XXX — Left wing
CROMWELL

THE BATTLE OF MARSTON MOOR

2 July 1644, viewed from the south-west. Early evening. Sir Thomas Fairfax's Allied right wing Horse are disorganised by rough ground and crushed by Goring's Royalist Horse. Early success by the Allied Foot turns to disaster as Royalist reserves shatter part of the Allied main body of infantry and Royalist Horse attack from the flank. It falls to Cromwell's Ironsides, with the vital support of Scots troopers, to defeat Rupert's Horse and to ride across the battlefield to stave off defeat.

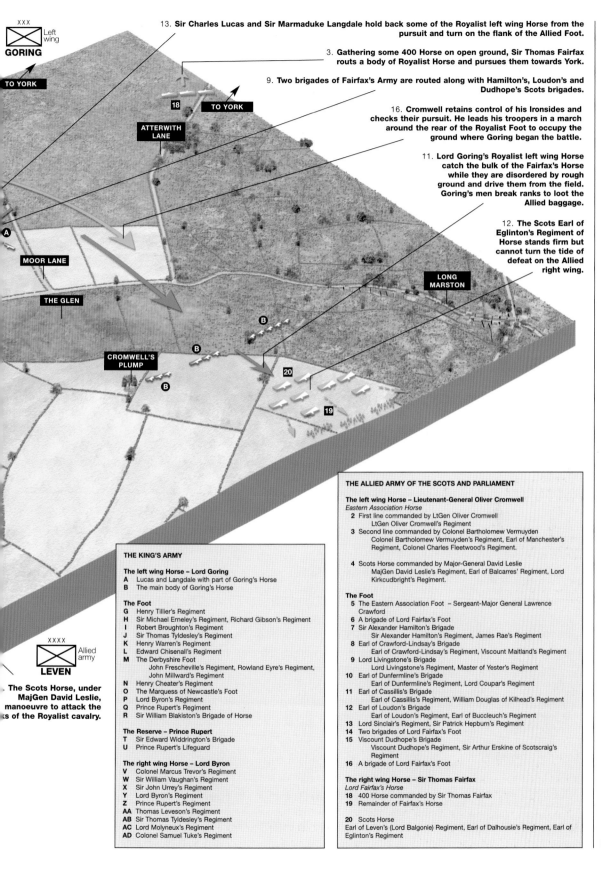

13. Sir Charles Lucas and Sir Marmaduke Langdale hold back some of the Royalist left wing Horse from the pursuit and turn on the flank of the Allied Foot.

3. Gathering some 400 Horse on open ground, Sir Thomas Fairfax routs a body of Royalist Horse and pursues them towards York.

9. Two brigades of Fairfax's Army are routed along with Hamilton's, Loudon's and Dudhope's Scots brigades.

16. Cromwell retains control of his Ironsides and checks their pursuit. He leads his troopers in a march around the rear of the Royalist Foot to occupy the ground where Goring began the battle.

11. Lord Goring's Royalist left wing Horse catch the bulk of the Fairfax's Horse while they are disordered by rough ground and drive them from the field. Goring's men break ranks to loot the Allied baggage.

12. The Scots Earl of Eglinton's Regiment of Horse stands firm but cannot turn the tide of defeat on the Allied right wing.

XXX
GORING Left wing

TO YORK

18

TO YORK

ATTERWITH LANE

MOOR LANE

THE GLEN

LONG MARSTON

CROMWELL'S PLUMP

20

19

XXXX
LEVEN Allied army

The Scots Horse, under MajGen David Leslie, manoeuvre to attack the ...s of the Royalist cavalry.

THE KING'S ARMY

The left wing Horse – Lord Goring
A Lucas and Langdale with part of Goring's Horse
B The main body of Goring's Horse

The Foot
G Henry Tillier's Regiment
H Sir Michael Erneley's Regiment, Richard Gibson's Regiment
I Robert Broughton's Regiment
J Sir Thomas Tyldesley's Regiment
K Henry Warren's Regiment
L Edward Chisenall's Regiment
M The Derbyshire Foot
    John Frescheville's Regiment, Rowland Eyre's Regiment, John Millward's Regiment
N Henry Cheater's Regiment
O The Marquess of Newcastle's Foot
P Lord Byron's Regiment
Q Prince Rupert's Regiment
R Sir William Blakiston's Brigade of Horse

The Reserve – Prince Rupert
T Sir Edward Widdrington's Brigade
U Prince Rupert's Lifeguard

The right wing Horse – Lord Byron
V Colonel Marcus Trevor's Regiment
W Sir William Vaughan's Regiment
X Sir John Urrey's Regiment
Y Lord Byron's Regiment
Z Prince Rupert's Regiment
AA Thomas Leveson's Regiment
AB Sir Thomas Tyldesley's Regiment
AC Lord Molyneux's Regiment
AD Colonel Samuel Tuke's Regiment

THE ALLIED ARMY OF THE SCOTS AND PARLIAMENT

The left wing Horse – Lieutenant-General Oliver Cromwell
Eastern Association Horse
2 First line commanded by LtGen Oliver Cromwell
    LtGen Oliver Cromwell's Regiment
3 Second line commanded by Colonel Bartholomew Vermuyden
    Colonel Bartholomew Vermuyden's Regiment, Earl of Manchester's Regiment, Colonel Charles Fleetwood's Regiment.

4 Scots Horse commanded by Major-General David Leslie
    MajGen David Leslie's Regiment, Earl of Balcarres' Regiment, Lord Kirkcudbright's Regiment.

The Foot
5 The Eastern Association Foot – Sergeant-Major General Lawrence Crawford
6 A brigade of Lord Fairfax's Foot
7 Sir Alexander Hamilton's Brigade
    Sir Alexander Hamilton's Regiment, James Rae's Regiment
8 Earl of Crawford-Lindsay's Brigade
    Earl of Crawford-Lindsay's Regiment, Viscount Maitland's Regiment
9 Lord Livingstone's Brigade
    Lord Livingstone's Regiment, Master of Yester's Regiment
10 Earl of Dunfermline's Brigade
    Earl of Dunfermline's Regiment, Lord Coupar's Regiment
11 Earl of Cassillis's Brigade
    Earl of Cassillis's Regiment, William Douglas of Kilhead's Regiment
12 Earl of Loudon's Brigade
    Earl of Loudon's Regiment, Earl of Buccleuch's Regiment
13 Lord Sinclair's Regiment, Sir Patrick Hepburn's Regiment
14 Two brigades of Lord Fairfax's Foot
15 Viscount Dudhope's Brigade
    Viscount Dudhope's Regiment, Sir Arthur Erskine of Scotscraig's Regiment
16 A brigade of Lord Fairfax's Foot

The right wing Horse – Sir Thomas Fairfax
Lord Fairfax's Horse
18 400 Horse commanded by Sir Thomas Fairfax
19 Remainder of Fairfax's Horse

20 Scots Horse
    Earl of Leven's (Lord Balgonie) Regiment, Earl of Dalhousie's Regiment, Earl of Eglinton's Regiment

The Marston Moor monument has been repaired recently and a new plinth constructed, just visible to the right, which will hold a plan of the battlefield.

John Lambert commanded Sir Thomas Fairfax's second line of cavalry but was unable to keep his inexperienced troopers in order.

from land crossed by ditches and hedges. Cromwell's divisions retained their order and Byron may have considered that the momentum to be gained from a counter-charge outweighed the support of a single volley of musket fire at long range.

Byron's first charge failed to halt the Parliamentarians and Stuart Reid has suggested that the Regiment of Horse posted on the left of Byron's front line may have been unable to charge due to the presence of the two regiments of Foot placed in a forward position by the ditch. Byron was able to recover from this first setback by re-forming on his supporting line while the unengaged squadrons from his first line and the 'refused' regiment of Samuel Tuke charged into the exposed flank of Cromwell's tightly packed formation.

Prince Rupert now arrived to add his Lifeguard and the small brigade of Sir Edward Widdrington to what was becoming the decisive cavalry engagement of the Civil War. The contest was finely balanced with both sides having committed their reserves and expended their pistols. Watson describes the fighting: 'Cromwells own division had a hard pull of it: for they were charged by Ruperts bravest men, both in Front and flank: they stood at the swords point a pretty while, hacking at one another: but at last (it so pleased God) he brake through them, scattering them before him like a little dust.'

Watson's report was written very shortly after the battle and he concentrates on the actions of Manchester's army almost to the exclusion of all other Allied involvement. In particular he fails to mention the decisive contribution of the Scots Horse under David Leslie, who had been positioned in support of Cromwell's Horse. Leslie had led his men against the exposed flank of the advanced Royalist Foot, but seeing Cromwell's Horse attacked in the flank he in turn fell on the exposed flank of the Royalist Horse. This intervention tipped the balance and the Royalist horsemen in the rear ranks, seeing their comrades cut down by the advancing Parliamentarians and Scots, turned their horses and rode for York with all speed.

Rupert was caught up in the rout and was forced to abandon command of his army to escape capture. Parliamentarian pamphleteers eagerly recounted how Rupert was forced to hide in a field of beans and depicted the Prince who had haunted them as the invincible commander of the King's Horse, humiliated and face down in the dirt.

With both sides having won decisive victories on their respective left wing the battle had swung around like a revolving door. On the Allied left Cromwell's cavalry paused to re-form, their discipline overcoming the desire to plunder their fleeing opponents. On the left of the Allied Foot Manchester's Foot brigades had successfully crossed the ditch and were pushing back the Royalist Foot, who were disheartened by the defeat of Rupert and the Horse covering their flank. The centre and right of the Allied Foot had halted or were falling back as their right wing Horse streamed back over the ridge pursued by the Royalist Horse.

THE INFANTRY FIGHTING

In the centre of the Allied line a brigade of Lord Fairfax's Foot fell back in the face of a determined countercharge by Newcastle's Foot, who moved forwards into the gaps between the first line divisions of Tyldesley and the Irish. To their right the Scots Brigade commanded by Sandie Hamilton was swept back in confusion and carried away with it the supporting units in the second line, which broke and joined the flight.

Sir William Blakiston's Brigade of Horse had been positioned close behind the centre of the Royalist Foot with the intention of his exploiting just such an opportunity. Blakiston did not fail, and his horsemen cut a swathe through Parliamentarian and Scots Foot brigades, following up Fairfax's retreating men and roughly handling the Scots brigades of Erskine and Dudhope which both suffered casualties. Blakiston's small command had penetrated the final line of the Allied Foot, but the impetus of their charge had gone and they rode on to the crest of the ridge as a spent force.

Other gaps were appearing in the Allied line as units from the second line broke and ran. Lumsden reported to the Earl of Loudoun: 'These that ran away shew themselves most baselie. I comanding the battel was on the head of your Lordships regiment and Buccleuches; but they carried themselves not so as I could have wished, neither could I prevaile with them: For these that fled, never came to charge with the enemie, but were so possest with ane pannick fear, that they ran for an example to others, and no enemie following them.'

Lumsden now acted to plug the hole in the Allied line: 'These Briggads that failyied of the vane were presently supplied by Cassels, Cowper, Dumfermling, and some of Clydisdailes regiment, who were on the battell, and gained what they had lost.'

That Lumsden was able to recover the situation in the Allied centre was due to the courage of the men of Lord Lindsey's Brigade, who stood on the extreme left of the first line of the Allied Foot.

The Royalist Horse left wing had repeated the mistake they had made two years previously during the first battle of the civil wars fought at Edgehill in 1642. Defeating the Parliamentarian Horse they had dispersed in pursuit and had thrown away a decisive victory. At Edgehill only Sir Charles Lucas had kept his head and had formed a body of Horse around him to continue the fight. At Marston Moor Lucas repeated this feat and kept part of his brigade under his control when others rode off in pursuit of the fleeing Parliamentarians. Lucas now led his men against the flank of Lord Lindsey's Brigade of Scottish Foot.

With Newcastle's Foot to their front and Lucas's Horse to their flank the Scots regiments interlined their pikemen with musketeers and not satisfied with holding their ground they forced the Royalist Horse to retire. This gallant stand of Lindsey's Brigade continued for perhaps an hour with reinforcements being fed in to support them. At the third attack of the Royalist Horse, Lucas was unhorsed and captured and his cavalry force dispersed.

Lucas was not the only Royalist cavalry commander to have kept his command under control. Sir Marmaduke Langdale may not have taken part in the initial charge as he was free to launch an attack on the Allied Foot.

Langdale's attack reached the top of the ridge and rode on to the Allied baggage train. The impact of the attack can be measured by the fact that all three generals of the Allied army fled the field. Leven and Lord Fairfax did not return, but Manchester managed to gather together some 500 horsemen and return to the left wing of his army.

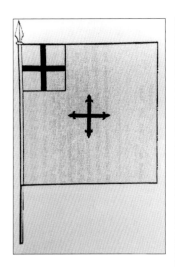

Lamplugh's Regiment of Foot. First Captain's colour. Yellow field, St George's Arms with a black cross patonce in the centre of the field. (artwork by Mike Seed courtesy Partizan Press)

Sir Thomas Tyldesley's personal Cornet of Horse. Red field, golden pelican and laurel wreath, red and gold fringe. The motto reads 'King and country deserve such love'. (artwork by Mike Seed courtesy Partizan Press)

CROMWELL'S IRONSIDES CHARGE PRINCE RUPERT'S HORSE (pages 66–67)

In the 17th century commanders were expected to lead their men into battle and the most famous general of the age, the Swedish king Gustavus Adolphus, had paid the ultimate price when he was shot and killed at the battle of Lutzen in 1632. Cromwell (1) was no stranger to the dangers of combat. At Winceby on 11 October 1643, Cromwell's horse was shot from under him and as he pulled himself free he was knocked over by the Royalist cavalryman Sir Ingram Hopton. Luckily Hopton was cut down before he could finish the kill and a fresh horse carried Cromwell out of harm's way. At Marston Moor Cromwell fought in the front line of his regiment and their charge resulted in an epic clash as Cromwell's men fought hand to hand with Prince Rupert's Horse 'at the swords point a pretty while, hacking one another'. At some point Cromwell received a wound to his neck, perhaps a burn from the muzzle of the pistol of one of his own men firing from the rank behind him. Here Cromwell sways in his saddle as the searing heat of the gunpowder blast burns his neck and his men look on anxiously to see if their leader will topple from his horse. Cromwell was taken to a house in Tockwith for his wound to be dressed. He returned to the battle against the Royalist Horse and 'at last (it so pleased God) he brake through

them, scattering them before him like a little dust'. Cromwell's equipment (based on that shown in the portrait of Colonel Nathaniel Fiennes by Mirevelt, probably dating from 1643) is similar to that of his troopers but of superior workmanship and materials. The breastplate (2) is pistol and carbine proof, with the back plate pistol proof. Unlike the ordinary trooper, Cromwell retains armour defending his hips (3). Although not shown here Cromwell also wore leg armour under the skirts of his buff coat (4) defending his thighs. The bridge gauntlet (5) worn on the left forearm features articulated metal plates to defend the hand and fingers while still allowing them freedom to move. The buff coat is made of the thickest parts of the hide and the sleeves are of two layers covering the upper arm down to below the elbow, with a decorated area cut out to allow the elbow to bend (6). Cromwell is armed with a pair of pistols fitted with English flintlocks (7). One pistol was to be fired just before the final charge with drawn swords and the other reserved for pursuit or retreat. Cromwell's helmet (8) is of a design known as a tri-bar that was worn by horsemen on both sides during the civil wars. Such helmets left little of the head unprotected, but the trooper who rides alongside Cromwell shows how a small area of the neck could be exposed (9) and it is this that led to Cromwell's wound at Marston Moor. (Graham Turner)

From a hundred paces along Moor Lane, looking north, a hedge-line and ditch still cross the fields at the point where cultivated ground gave way to moorland. Wilstrop Wood can be seen in the distance.

This drawing, taken from a broadsheet of 1651, depicts the dress of a common soldier of the Scots army as it would have appeared in 1644.

CROMWELL'S VICTORY

With the generals making their way from the battlefield, command of the Allied armies fell on the lieutenant- and major-generals. Sir Thomas Fairfax crossed the battlefield and reached Cromwell to deliver news of the disaster that had overtaken this own command. Some five or six troops under John Lambert and two squadrons of Balgonie's Scots Horse also fought their way through to join Cromwell.

Cromwell now faced the kind of responsibility that comes to few subordinate officers. The senior generals were nowhere to be found. Sir Thomas Fairfax had lost his command and the Foot Brigades had been routed or fought to a standstill. Cromwell's cavalry was now the only disengaged force that remained under effective command amongst the three Allied armies. Did Cromwell hesitate?

After the battle, Cromwell's political enemies circulated stories that he had not played a significant part in the victory at Marston Moor. Denzil Holles MP recorded in his Memoirs: 'I have several times heard it from Lawrence Crawford's own mouth that when the whole army at Marston Moor was in a fair possibility to be utterly routed, and a great part of it running, he saw the whole body of horse of that Brigade standing still, and, to his seeming, doubtful which way to charge, backward or forward, when he came up to them in a great passion, reviling them with the name of poltroons and cowards, and asked them if they would stand still and see the day lost? Whereupon Cromwell shewed himself, and in a pitiful voice said, "Major-General, what shall I do?" he (begging pardon for what he said, not knowing he was there, towards whom he knew his distance as to his superior officer) told him, "Sir, if you charge not all is lost." Cromwell answered he was wounded (his great wound being a little burn in the neck by accidental going off behind him of one of his soldiers' pistols). Then

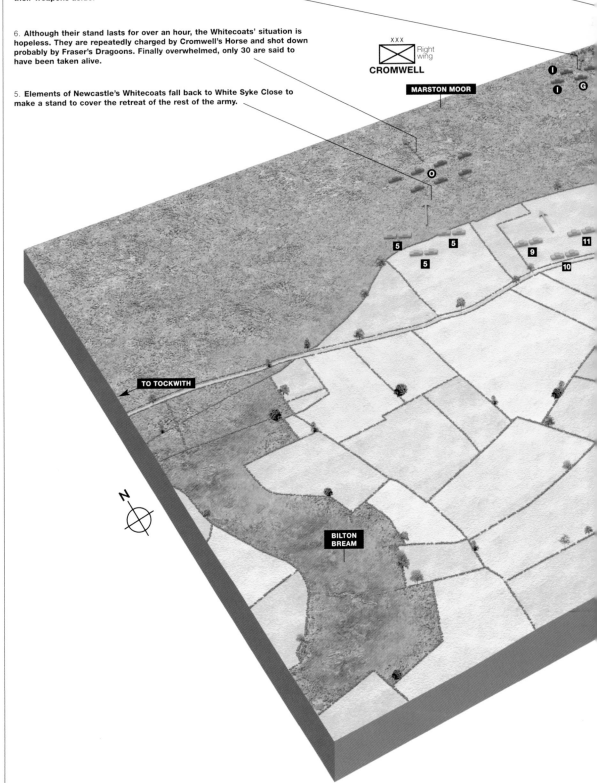

3. With their cavalry gone the Royalist Foot can do little but attempt to retire in some order. Many turn and flee, casting their weapons aside.

4. The bulk of the Royalist infantry flees towards York. A brigade of 'greencoats', probably veterans from Ireland, is charged down and routed as it retreats.

6. Although their stand lasts for over an hour, the Whitecoats' situation is hopeless. They are repeatedly charged by Cromwell's Horse and shot down probably by Fraser's Dragoons. Finally overwhelmed, only 30 are said to have been taken alive.

5. Elements of Newcastle's Whitecoats fall back to White Syke Close to make a stand to cover the retreat of the rest of the army.

x x x
Right wing
CROMWELL

MARSTON MOOR

O

5   5
5
9   11
10

TO TOCKWITH

N

BILTON BREAM

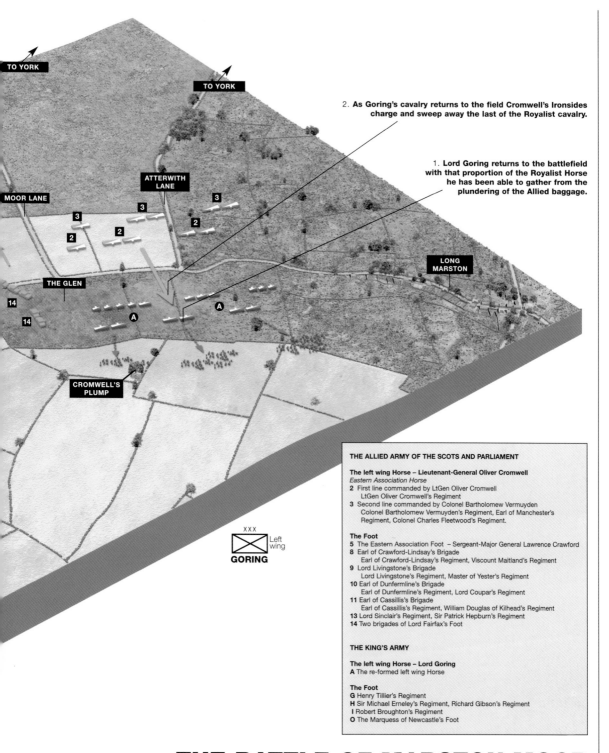

TO YORK

TO YORK

2. As Goring's cavalry returns to the field Cromwell's Ironsides charge and sweep away the last of the Royalist cavalry.

1. Lord Goring returns to the battlefield with that proportion of the Royalist Horse he has been able to gather from the plundering of the Allied baggage.

ATTERWITH LANE

MOOR LANE

LONG MARSTON

THE GLEN

CROMWELL'S PLUMP

XXX
Left wing
GORING

THE ALLIED ARMY OF THE SCOTS AND PARLIAMENT

The left wing Horse – Lieutenant-General Oliver Cromwell
Eastern Association Horse
2 First line commanded by LtGen Oliver Cromwell
   LtGen Oliver Cromwell's Regiment
3 Second line commanded by Colonel Bartholomew Vermuyden
   Colonel Bartholomew Vermuyden's Regiment, Earl of Manchester's
   Regiment, Colonel Charles Fleetwood's Regiment

The Foot
5 The Eastern Association Foot – Sergeant-Major General Lawrence Crawford
8 Earl of Crawford-Lindsay's Brigade
   Earl of Crawford-Lindsay's Regiment, Viscount Maitland's Regiment
9 Lord Livingstone's Brigade
   Lord Livingstone's Regiment, Master of Yester's Regiment
10 Earl of Dunfermline's Brigade
   Earl of Dunfermline's Regiment, Lord Coupar's Regiment
11 Earl of Cassillis's Brigade
   Earl of Cassillis's Regiment, William Douglas of Kilhead's Regiment
13 Lord Sinclair's Regiment, Sir Patrick Hepburn's Regiment
14 Two brigades of Lord Fairfax's Foot

THE KING'S ARMY

The left wing Horse – Lord Goring
A The re-formed left wing Horse

The Foot
G Henry Tillier's Regiment
H Sir Michael Erneley's Regiment, Richard Gibson's Regiment
I Robert Broughton's Regiment
O The Marquess of Newcastle's Foot

THE BATTLE OF MARSTON MOOR

2 July 1644, viewed from the south-west. Late evening. Goring's victorious Royalist Horse returns to the battlefield to find Cromwell's Horse ready to charge. Cromwell sweeps all before him and turns to attack the unsupported Royalist Foot. The battle ends with the Allied forces disorganised and exhausted, but the Royalist Army has been driven from the field and destroyed as an effective fighting force.

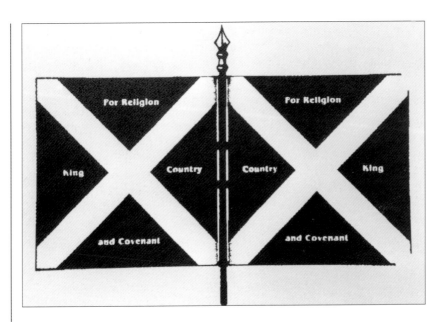

Crawford desired him to go off the field and, sending one away with him (who very readily followed wholesome advice), led them on himself, which was not the duty of his place, and as little for Cromwell's honour as it proved to be much for the advancement of his and his parties pernicious designs.'

Holles was a major figure in the political opposition to Cromwell and the religious Independents whom he championed, and it was in the interests of

Facing south from Moor Lane, the group of trees known as 'Cromwell's Plump' can be seen on the higher ridge. The dark line of the lower ridge can be seen running along the Allied position.

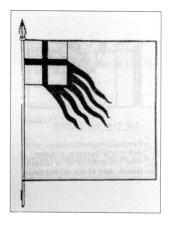

This unidentified Royalist colour was captured at Marston Moor. White field, red cross of St George, five black streams blazant. (artwork by Mike Seed courtesy Partizan Press)

'Cromwell's Plump' viewed from the road by the monument. The line of the lower ridge can just be made out showing the dip in the ridge which forms an entry to the 'Glen'.

Cromwell's opponents to belittle and denigrate the part he had played at Marston Moor. Major-General Crawford, who died in 1645, was also an outspoken opponent of Cromwell and his account is unlikely to have been unbiased.

Regardless of when Cromwell rejoined them, the Allied left wing Horse now set off in a semicircular march that took them around the rear of the still defiant Royalist Foot. They came to the place where the Royalist left wing Horse had stood at the start of the battle. It thus fell to the men of Goring and Langdale, returning from pillaging the Allied baggage train, to form up on the difficult ground which Fairfax's Horse had occupied at the start of the battle. The resulting clash was between unequal forces. The Royalists on broken ground, their numbers as much diminished by the lure of further plunder as by casualties, were no match for the re-formed ranks of Cromwell's command and a single charge swept them from the field of battle.

Bodies of disorganised Royalist Horse remained on the field well into the night for Sir Philip Monkton states that he met Sir John Urry with a group of perhaps 2,000 horsemen and stayed with them until midnight when they were ordered to withdraw to York.

THE WHITECOATS DEFIANT!

Stripped of support from their cavalry wings and reserve, the Royalist Foot now faced a hopeless struggle. Outflanked on their right by Manchester's Foot, with Scots Foot to their front and Horse closing in on their left flank and rear, there was little to do but fall back as best they could. A brigade of Greencoats, probably regiments from Ireland, fought stubbornly but was overrun. General King was able to organise a rearguard in the form of the sacrificial stand to the last of some part of

THE DEFIANT LAST STAND OF NEWCASTLE'S WHITECOATS
(pages 74–75)

Abandoned by their cavalry, the infantry of the Royalist army found themselves isolated in the midst of the wide-open space of Marston Moor. Many turned and fled, some threw down their weapons and pleaded that they were not truly Royalists but had been forcibly pressed into the service of the King. A brigade of green-coated Irish veterans were charged down and routed by Scots cavalry, but amidst the confusion many of the white-coated soldiers of Newcastle's Foot remained with their Colours. As the Royalist army broke up into a fleeing rabble, the Whitecoats fell back in good order to the ditched animal enclosure of White Syke Close, defiantly peppering their pursuers with musket shot. The Duchess of Newcastle, in her account of her husband's life, says that the Whitecoats 'showed such an extraordinary valour and courage in that action, that they were killed in rank and file.' Colonel James Somerville says of the Whitecoats 'when all their ammunition was spent, having refused quarters, every man fell in the same order and rank whereon he had fought'. However Somerville had long since departed the field in the company of the Earl of Leven in his flight to Leeds. William Lilley recorded the account of one Captain Camby who claimed to be the third or fourth horseman to break in

amongst the Whitecoats and says that he had never before encountered 'such resolute brave fellows, or whom he pitied so much'. It must be said that Camby was an actor and may have enhanced his own role in events. The last stand of Newcastle's Foot can have involved only a proportion of the men he brought to the battle that day. John Barratt has suggested that it may have been Newcastle's own Regiment of Foot that formed the defiant rearguard and a possible design of one of their standards is depicted here (1). Raised in 1642, many men of the regiment were veterans of the hard fighting at Piercebridge that year and Wakefield and Adwalton Moor in 1643. Newcastle's men had refused to surrender at Wakefield when the town had fallen to the Parliamentarian forces of Sir Thomas Fairfax and they had fought a bloody battle at push of pike at Adwalton Moor, charging against a force mainly of musketeers. The Whitecoats would have formed with their musketeers (2) firing and loading, crouching beneath the protection of pikemen holding their pikes at the 'charge' (3) and at 'charge for horse' (4). This gallant stand gave many of their comrades the chance to reach York in safety, but their resistance could not endure against the fire of Scots Dragoons and the swords of Cromwell's Ironsides (5) and it is said that only 30 survived to be taken prisoner. (Graham Turner)

The higher and lower ridges running off to the west towards Cromwell's position.

Cornet of a troop of Sir Thomas Fairfax's Regiment. (Courtesy of Partizan Press)

Newcastle's Whitecoats. The most famous account comes from William Lilley, who heard it from an actor called Camby, who claimed to have fought in the attack on the Whitecoats: 'this sole regiment, after the day was lost, having got into a small parcel of ground ditched in, and not of easy access to horse, would take no quarter, and by mere valour for one whole hour kept the troops of horse from entering amongst them at near push of pike; but when the horse did enter they would have no quarter, but fought it out till there was not thirty of them living; those whose hap it was to be beaten down upon the ground, as the troopers came near them, though they could not rise for their wounds, yet were so desperate as to get either a pike or sword a piece of them, and to gore the troopers' horses as they came over them or passed by …'

An eyewitness account left by Lieutenant-Colonel James Somerville, a Scots officer who attended Leven's army as a non-combatant, says the Parliamentarian Horse: 'falls in upon the naked flanks of the prince's main battalion of foot, carrying them down with great violence ; neither met they with any great resistance, until they came to the Marquis of Newcastle his battalion of white coats, who first peppering them soundly with their shot, when they came to charge stoutly bore them up with their pikes, that they could not enter to break them. Here the parliament horse of that wing received their greatest loss, and a stop for some time to their hoped-for-victory, and that only by the stout resistance of this gallant battalion, which consisted of near of four thousand foot, until at length a Scots regiment of Dragoons, commanded by Colonel Frizeall, with other two, was brought to open then upon some hand, which at length they did; when all their ammunition was spent, having refused quarters, every man fell in the same order and rank wherein he had fought.'

ABOVE **Once open moor, the main area of the infantry fighting has been transformed into rich plough land.**

OPPOSITE, TOP **The area occupied by Fairfax's Allied right wing, still somewhat more enclosed than the main ridge. This picture was taken from the top of the lower ridge and in the foreground the Glen can be seen to be a large bowl of low ground between the ridges where Sir Philip Monckton found 2,000 disorganised Royalist Horse at the end of the battle. From this viewpoint one can comprehend why they would not have been seen by troops on the moor.**

OPPOSITE, BOTTOM **The view over Rupert's positions from the lower ridge looking north. The moor has been drained and is now agricultural land. Wilstrop Wood is seen in the left background and the monument and Moor Lane are in the right foreground.**

The end of the battle

In the darkness the last stand of the Whitecoats marked the end of Royalist resistance on Marston Moor. Rupert's actions after the defeat of his Horse are uncertain, but he was among the last to return to York. In a brief meeting with Newcastle he discovered that Newcastle intended to abandon the Royalist cause and to seek exile overseas. Rupert remained determined to fight on. Slingsby describes the day after the battle: 'The Prince marched out the next morning with the remaining horse, and as many footmen as he could horse, leaving the rest in York. Thus were we left at York out of all hope of relief, the town much distracted, every one ready to abandon her.' Knowing that its fall was inevitable, the Allies did not hurry to make any attempt on the city and Sir Thomas Glemham surrendered York on 16 July. With the exception of isolated garrisons the northern part of the Kingdom of England was lost to the King.

Casualties

Simeon Ash, Manchester's chaplain, described the scene after the battle: 'That night we kept the field, when the Bodies of the dead were stripped. In the morning, there was a mortifying object to behold, when the naked bodies of thousands lay upon the ground, and many not altogether dead.'

Most of the contemporary narratives agree with Ash in enumerating the casualties: 'Wee judge that about three thousand of the Enemies were slaine ; but the Countreymen (who were commanded to bury the corpes) tell us they have buried foure thousand one hundred and fifty bodies.'

A Full Relation ... adds: 'The losse upon our part, blessed be God, is not great, being only of one Lieutenant-colonell, some few Captaines, and not 300 common Souldiers.'

A rough total of 1,500 prisoners including Sir Charles Lucas, Major-General Porter and Major-General Tilliard fell into the hands of the Allies. Manchester captured: 'ten pieces of ordinance, one case of Drakes, foure thousand and five hundred muskets, forty barrels of Powder, three tun of great and small Bullet, eight hundred Pikes, besides Swords, Bandileers, etc.' *A Full Relation* ... says that in addition to 25 pieces of artillery and 130 barrels of powder were captured 'above an hundred Colours and ten thousand arms besides two Waggons of Carbines and Pistols of spare Armes.'

The personal nature of the defeat for Prince Rupert was symbolised in the death of his pet poodle (the breed at this time was a hunting dog) named 'Boy', which had been given to him when he was a prisoner in the Imperial castle of Linz. Along with his dog Rupert's reputation for invincibility died at Marston Moor.

AFTERMATH

In his letter of 14 June King Charles had warned Prince Rupert that he must relieve York, defeat the Allied armies and march south to save the King's main Oxford army from destruction at the hands of the combined Parliamentarian armies of the Earl of Essex and Sir William Waller. The King foretold that should York surrender, his crown would be as good as lost 'unless supported by your sudden march to me; and a miraculous conquest in the South'. Rupert had failed in all his endeavours and York was in the hands of the victorious Allied army.

The victory of Marston Moor should have marked the turning point in the war and enabled the overwhelming strength of the Parliamentarian and Scots armies to close in on the King. Instead a miracle, in the shape of quarrelling Parliamentarian commanders, intervened to give King Charles an unexpected run of victories.

After the defeat of the Royalist right wing Horse, Rupert was forced to hide in a bean field. Boy, Rupert's poodle, is depicted as a casualty amongst Popish idols.

THE AFTERMATH OF MARSTON MOOR, JUNE–SEPTEMBER 1644

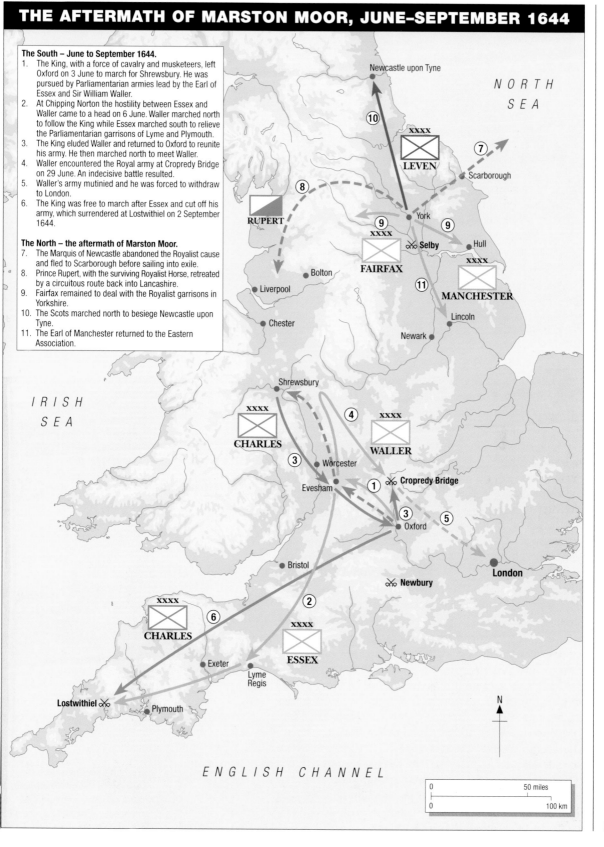

The South – June to September 1644.
1. The King, with a force of cavalry and musketeers, left Oxford on 3 June to march for Shrewsbury. He was pursued by Parliamentarian armies lead by the Earl of Essex and Sir William Waller.
2. At Chipping Norton the hostility between Essex and Waller came to a head on 6 June. Waller marched north to follow the King while Essex marched south to relieve the Parliamentarian garrisons of Lyme and Plymouth.
3. The King eluded Waller and returned to Oxford to reunite his army. He then marched north to meet Waller.
4. Waller encountered the Royal army at Cropredy Bridge on 29 June. An indecisive battle resulted.
5. Waller's army mutinied and he was forced to withdraw to London.
6. The King was free to march after Essex and cut off his army, which surrendered at Lostwithiel on 2 September 1644.

The North – the aftermath of Marston Moor.
7. The Marquis of Newcastle abandoned the Royalist cause and fled to Scarborough before sailing into exile.
8. Prince Rupert, with the surviving Royalist Horse, retreated by a circuitous route back into Lancashire.
9. Fairfax remained to deal with the Royalist garrisons in Yorkshire.
10. The Scots marched north to besiege Newcastle upon Tyne.
11. The Earl of Manchester returned to the Eastern Association.

Newcastle upon Tyne

NORTH SEA

LEVEN

Scarborough

RUPERT

York

Hull

FAIRFAX

Selby

Bolton

MANCHESTER

Liverpool

Chester

Lincoln

Newark

IRISH SEA

Shrewsbury

CHARLES

WALLER

Worcester

Evesham

Cropredy Bridge

Oxford

Bristol

London

Newbury

CHARLES

ESSEX

Exeter

Lyme Regis

Lostwithiel

Plymouth

ENGLISH CHANNEL

N

0   50 miles
0   100 km

The King's strategy for 1644 was that the Oxford army should stand on the defensive to await Rupert's return from the relief of York. However in early June the King marched out of the city with a fast-moving force of some 5,000 Horse and 2,500 musketeers, aiming to lead the Parliamentarians away from Oxford and outdistance their pursuit. By 6 June the King had reached Worcester, with the armies of Essex and Waller some way distant at Chipping Norton. Unknown to the Royalists the animosity between Essex and Waller had boiled over and the former had decided to take his army to relieve besieged Parliamentarian garrisons in Dorset and Devon. Waller was ordered to keep the King under a close watch. On 12 June the King's army reached Bewdley and Charles established himself at Tickhill Manor for a two-day Council of War.

When he wrote his letter to Rupert on 14 June, King Charles believed himself to be still pursued by the combined armies of Essex and Waller. The Royalist commanders decided to march back to Oxford to re-form their field army. The Royalist Horse was stationed at Bridgnorth, implying that the King's next move would be to the important Royalist recruiting centre of Shrewsbury. Accordingly Waller placed his army at Stourbridge to cover a march to the north by the Royalist army.

In fact on 15 June the Royalist musketeers boarded boats and moved quickly downriver to Worcester, where they were joined by the Horse. By 16 June the Royalists were at Evesham, closer to Oxford than Waller, who remained at Stourbridge. As the Royalists marched they broke down the bridges behind them. On 18 June the Royalists reached Witney just outside Oxford and on the following day the Oxford army was reunited. The King now moved his army to Buckingham, where he spent several days re-supplying his stocks of ammunition and powder.

While the Royal army was making its escape back to Oxford, Sir William Waller at last realised that he had been duped and set off in pursuit. The

Rupert's pet poodle 'Boy' was a favourite target for the propagandists from early in the war. Here Toby's good Parliamentarian dog Pepper confronts a Royalist Poodle intended to be Boy.

Cornet of Lambert's Horse in 1644. Red field, green mound, golden column, white scroll. (artwork by Mike Seed courtesy Partizan Press)

The death of Rupert's poodle at Marston Moor was celebrated in a pamphlet called 'A Dogs Elegy or Rupert's Tears' which suggests the dog was his satanic 'familiar'. The text reads 'Sad Cavaliers, Rupert invites you all That doe survive, to his Dogs Funerall Close-mourners are the Witch, Pope, & Devill, That much lament your late befallen evill'.

Royalist deception had been so effective that Waller set off in the wrong direction seeking his adversary at Gloucester. However, the Committee of Both Kingdoms soon informed Waller that the King and his full army were at Buckingham and, so they feared, about to descend on the Eastern Association. Waller was ordered to intercept the King and on 28 June he camped at Hanwell near Banbury. By this time the King had marched to Brackley in Northamptonshire and when news of Waller's arrival reached him he set out to protect his garrison at Banbury.

A Victorian representation of the defeated Royalists streaming back into York after Marston Moor. Fearful that pursuing Parliamentarians would enter the city, the garrison commander closed the gates against all but troops from the garrison.

Personal standard of Sir Thomas Fairfax. Dark blue field with darker blue acanthus pattern and blue and white fringe. (artwork by Mike Seed courtesy Partizan Press)

Cornet of the Troop of Horse of Ferdinando, Lord Fairfax. White field, red and gold crown, blue and gold mitre, gold-hilted sword. Motto: 'Long live the King and death to bad Government' (artwork by Mike Seed courtesy Partizan Press)

Both armies found strong defensive positions to the south-west of Banbury and the Royalists were easily able to repulse a Parliamentarian attack. The Royalists marched north to Daventry, forcing Waller to follow them. On 29 June at Cropredy Bridge, Waller saw a chance to attack part of the Royalist column that had become strung out on the march. His attack failed and Waller's forces suffered a rebuff, but not a defeat. Waller's eye for ground enabled him to form up in another strong defensive position where he awaited Major-General Browne with a Parliamentarian force of 4,500 men.

The Royalists decided that they could no longer face Waller and they set off for Evesham, reaching it on the night of 3 July. Here reports of a great Royalist victory outside York first reached them and bonfires blazed in celebration throughout the night. Their joy was short-lived for it quickly became clear that the reports dispatched after the Royalist left

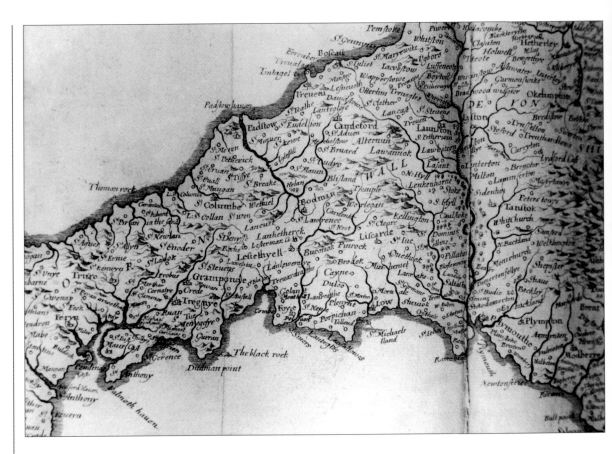

Hollar's map published in 1644 shows Lostwithiel, scene of the destruction of the army of the Earl of Essex as 'Lestethyell'. By marching into Cornwall, Essex had made the isolation of his army a simple matter for the Royalists.

wing had achieved its success had told less than the whole story and that the armies of Rupert and Newcastle had been destroyed. The King determined to march into the West Country, towards Exeter, to rejoin his Queen and see what could be salvaged of his seemingly hopeless cause.

As the King gloomily considered the prospect of defeat, the miracle that he had cautioned Rupert would be needed now began to take shape. Waller had combined forces with Browne at Towcester but a mutinous spirit had grown up amongst the London Trained Bands that formed a substantial part of his infantry. The men of the Trained Bands found themselves far from home in a campaign of marching hither and thither in the footsteps of the wandering King. One Trained Band regiment marched off carrying the body of their colonel, who had died of sickness, back to London. Desertion became endemic and Waller's army began to dissolve around him. By 26 July Waller was back in London and the King was free to march where he would.

The Earl of Essex had relieved Lyme in mid-June and Plymouth on 18 July. At the approach of the King, Essex marched into Cornwall and sought to contact the Parliamentarian fleet in the harbours around Lostwithiel in the hope that they would be able to sail his infantry back to London, and that his cavalry could slip through the Royalist lines. Essex's hopes of rescue from the sea were confounded by adverse weather that kept the fleet away from the Cornish coast.

On 14 August, at Bridgewater, the Royalists defeated a force of 2,000 Parliamentarian Horse, preventing their marching on to reinforce Essex. Knowing that their enemy was trapped and growing weaker by the day

Following the second battle of
Newbury in 1644, King Charles
left his artillery and wounded
soldiers with the nearby Royalist
garrison at Donnington Castle.

the Royalists delayed their attacks until 21 August, driving Essex's forces
back into a shrinking bridgehead. The Earl of Essex escaped in a small
boat while his cavalry, under the redoubtable Sir William Balfour, fought
their way to Plymouth. It was left to Sir Philip Skippon to surrender the
infantry of Essex's army, which marched away without its arms.

On 30 September at South Perrot, near Chard in Somerset, King
Charles met with Prince Rupert for the first time since the disaster
at Marston Moor and the victories of Cropredy Bridge and Lostwithiel.
The King's opinion of his own military abilities had been dangerously
enhanced, but his objectives were modest as he aimed only to re-supply his
garrisons at Banbury, Basing House and Donnington Castle near Newbury.

Parliament feared a full-scale attack on London. Following the
surrender of York, the Scots had marched north to besiege Newcastle,
Fairfax remained in Yorkshire to reduce Royalist garrisons and Manchester
had returned to the Eastern Association.

Fortunately for the Parliamentarians the King was in no hurry and it was not until 2 October that he reached Sherborne in Dorset. Waller was then at Salisbury, Manchester had only reached Reading and Essex remained re-equipping his battered army at Portsmouth. On 22 October the King relieved Donnington Castle.

The Parliamentarians formed a plan that appears to have been intended to separate the feuding Parliamentarian commanders as much as to defeat the King. Manchester remained to the east of Newbury with his infantry while Waller, with Skippon commanding Essex's infantry and Cromwell the bulk of the Eastern Association cavalry, set out on an overnight flanking march to fall on Newbury from the west. On 27 October the attacks were launched late in the day with only two hours before the winter's daylight failed. The attacks were badly co-ordinated and the Royalists were able to hold their ground. Fearing that the next day would bring the overwhelming Parliamentarian strength down on them, the Royalists marched out through the gap between the Parliamentarian armies, leaving their artillery and casualties at Donnington Castle as they passed.

One final humiliation remained for the Parliamentarians. On 9 November the Royalist army led by Rupert returned to Donnington Castle, recovered its artillery unmolested and formed up on open ground to offer battle. Manchester argued against accepting battle and the King was able to march away to winter quarters as master of the field.

In response Parliament set out to ensure that its armies were commanded by competent, professional soldiers and passed a Self Denying Ordinance prohibiting all members of the House of Commons and House of Lords from holding military command. Oliver Cromwell as hero of Marston Moor, the victory that had enabled the Parliamentarian cause to survive the defeats of 1644, was specifically exempted from the Ordinance. Thus, thanks to Marston Moor, Cromwell alone retained both military and political influence in the English State and was to use his unique position to succeed King Charles as king in all but name.

ORDERS OF BATTLE

THE ALLIED ARMIES OF THE SCOTS AND PARLIAMENT

ARMY OF THE EASTERN ASSOCIATION
Lord General: Earl of Manchester
Lieutenant-General of the Horse: Oliver Cromwell
Sergeant-Major General of the Foot: Lawrence Crawford
The Train of Artillery: LtGen Thomas Hammond

The Horse

Earl of Manchester (Col Algernon Sidney)	11 trps	(c.700)
LtGen Oliver Cromwell (LtCol E. Whalley)	14 trps	(c.800)
Col Bartholomew Vermuyden	5 trps	(c.350)
Col Charles Fleetwood	6 trps	(c.400)

The Dragoons

LtCol John Lilburne	5 coys	(c500)

The Foot

Earl of Manchester (LtCol Clifton)	18 coys	(c.1,500)
MajGen L. Crawford (LtCol W. Hamilton)	8 coys	(c.850)
Col Sir Michael Hobart	9 coys	(c.900)
Col Francis Russell's	10 coys	(c.1,000)
Col Edward Montagu's	10 coys	(c.750)
Col John Pickering's	10 coys	(c.750)

THE SCOTS ARMY – The Army of the Solemn League and Covenant
Lord General: Earl of Leven
Lieutenant-General of the Horse: David Leslie
Lieutenant-General of the Foot: William Baillie
Sergeant-Major General of the Foot: Sir James Lumsden

The Horse

Earl of Leven (Lord Balgonie)	8 troop	(c.350)
Earl of Dalhousie	7 troops	(c.350)
Earl of Eglinton	7 troops	(c.350)
MajGen David Leslie	8 troops	(c.350)
Earl of Balcarres	8 troops	(c.350)
Lord Kirkcudbright	8 troops	(c.350)

The Dragoons

Hugh Fraser	6 companies	(c.500)

The Foot
Lieutenant-General William Baillie's Brigades
Earl of Crawford-Lindsey's Brigade

Earl of Crawford-Lindsay ⎤	
Viscount Maitland ⎦	(c.1,500)

Sir Alexander Hamilton's Brigade

Sir Alexander Hamilton ⎤	
James Rae's Regiment ⎦	(c.1,500)

Sergeant-Major General Sir James Lumsden's Brigades
Earl of Loudon's Brigade

Earl of Loudon ⎤	
Earl of Buccleuch ⎦	(c.1,500)

Earl of Cassillis's Brigade

Earl of Cassillis ⎤	
William Douglas of Kilhead ⎦	(c.1,500)

Earl of Dunfermline's Brigade

Earl of Dunfermline ⎤	
Lord Coupar ⎦	(c.1,500)

Lord Livingstone's Brigade

Lord Livingstone ⎤	
Master of Yester ⎦	(c.1,500)

Viscount Dudhope's Brigade

Viscount Dudhope ⎤	
Sir Arthur Erskine of Scotscraig ⎦	(c.1,500)

Lord Sinclair's Regiment	(c.750)

The Train of Artillery: Sir Alexander Hamilton
(only the lighter guns were present at the battle)

Brass demicannons	8
Brass culverin	1
Brass quarter-cannons	3
Brass demi-cannon	48
Iron demi-cannon	9
Frames	88

ARMY OF FERDINANDO LORD FAIRFAX
Lord General: Ferdinando Lord Fairfax
Lieutenant-General of the Horse: Sir Thomas Fairfax

The Horse (3,000 Horse in 80 troops)
Lord Fairfax's Regiment
Sir Thomas Fairfax's Regiment
Charles Fairfax's Regiment
Hugh Bethell's Regiment
John Lambert's Regiment
Lionel Copley's Regiment
Francis Boynton's Regiment
Sir Thomas Norcliff's Regiment

The Dragoons

Thomas Morgan	(c.500)

The Foot (3,000 soldiers in four brigades)
Lord Fairfax's Regiment
John Bright's Regiment
Sir William Constable's Regiment
Francis Lascelles's Regiment
Robert Overton's Regiment
Ralph Ashton's Regiment
George Dodding's Regiment
Alexander Rigby's Regiment

THE KING'S ARMIES

ARMY OF THE MARQUIS OF NEWCASTLE
Lord General: Marquis of Newcastle
(James King, Lord Eythin as military adviser)
Lieutenant-General of the Horse: Lord George Goring
Sergeant-Major General of the Foot: Sir Francis Mackworth

The Horse

Sir Charles Lucas's Brigade	(c.1,100)
Sir Richard Dacre's Brigade	(c.800)
Sir William Blakiston's Brigade	(c.500)
Sir Edward Widdrington's Brigade	(c.400)
Col Samuel Tuke's Regiment	(c.200)
Col Sir Francis Carnaby's Regiment	(c.200)
Commissary-General George Porter's Troop	(c.60)
Marquis of Newcastle's Lifeguard	(c.40)
(Sir Thomas Metham)	

The Foot (3,000–4,000 soldiers in seven divisions)
Sir Philip Byron's Regiment
Cuthbert Conyers's Regiment
Lord Eythin's Regiment
Sir John Gerlington's Regiment
John Hilton's Regiment
Sir Richard Hutton's Regiment
Richard Kirkebride's Regiment
Posthumus Kirton's Regiment
Sir William Lambton's Regiment
John Lamplugh's Regiment
Sir Marmaduke Langdale's Regiment
Lord Mansfield's Regiment
Sir Thomas Metham's Regiment
Marquis of Newcastle's Regiment
Sir Arthur Basset's Regiment
Sir Charles Slingsby's Regiment
Sir Richard Strickland's Regiment
Charles Towneley's Regiment
Lord Widdrington's Regiment

York Garrison
Sir Thomas Glemham's Regiment
John Belasyse's Regiment
Sir Henry Slingsby's Regiment

ARMY OF PRINCE RUPERT OF THE RHINE
Lord General: Prince Rupert
Lieutenant-General of the Horse: John Lord Byron
Sergeant-Major General of the Foot: Henry Tillier

The Horse

Prince Rupert's Lifeguard	(c.150)
Prince Rupert's Regiment	(c.500)
Lord Byron's Regiment	(c.500)
Col Marcus Trevor's Regiment	(c.300)
Sir John Urrey's Regiment	(c.400)
Sir William Vaughan's Regiment	(c.200)
Lord Molyneux's Regiment	(c.300)
Sir Thomas Tyldesley's Regiment	(c.300)
Rowland Eyre's Regiment	(c.130)
John Frescheville's Regiment	(c.160)
Thomas Leveson's Regiment	(c.200)

Dragoons

Henry Washington	(c.500)

The Foot
LtCol John Russell's Brigade (Thomas Napier)

Prince Rupert's Regiment	(1,000)
Lord Byron's Regiment	(c.500)
Henry Warren's Regiment	(c.500)
Sir Michael Erneley's Regiment	(c.250)
Richard Gibson's Regiment	(.250)
Henry Tillier's Regiment	(c.1000)
Robert Broughton's Regiment	(c.1,000)
Sir Thomas Tyldesley's Regiment	(c.1,000)
Edward Chisenall's Regiment	(c.1,000)
Henry Cheater's Regiment	(c.1,000)
John Frescheville's Regiment ⎫	
Rowland Eyre's Regiment ⎬	(c.500)
John Millward's Regiment ⎭	

The Train of Artillery
16–20 pieces of artillery

THE BATTLEFIELD TODAY

The B1224 Wetherby Road runs directly west from the York ring road, through Rufforth to Long Marston. A right turn at the *Star Public House* brings one onto the Tockwith Road that now marks the line of the track that in 1644 ran along the front of the Allied armies.

The obelisk monument to the battle stands next to the track known as Moor Lane. On the ridge opposite the monument can be seen the small group of trees known as 'Cromwell's Plump'. A farm track runs up towards the higher ridge and turns west as it crests the lower ridge. From this point the separation of the two ridges and the extent of the depression known as 'the Glen' can be seen clearly.

The moor has long since been transformed into ordinary farmland. The drainage ditch no longer runs across the fields but the hedge survives. A much-enlarged Wilstrop Wood forms a backdrop to the battlefield.

A visit to York and the evidence of its siege are an essential companion to the battlefield. The web site www.york.gov.uk offers an excellent virtual tour of the surviving walls, gates and fortifications of the city with a useful map for exploring on foot. The Castle museum has several exhibits from the Civil War including a fine display of cuirassier armour and weapons.

BIBLIOGRAPHY

On the battle of Marston Moor

Barratt, John, *The Battle for York, Marston Moor 1644* (Tempus Publications, 2002)

Evans, David, *The battle of Marston Moor 1644* (Stuart Press, 1994)

Newman, Peter, R., *The Battle of Marston Moor 1644* (Anthony Bird Publications, 1981)

Newman, Peter R., 'Marston Moor, 2 July 1644: the Sources and the site' *Borthwick papers No 53.* (University of York Borthwick Institute of Historical Research, 1978)

Reid, Stuart, *All the King's Armies, A Military History of the English Civil War 1642–1651* (Spellmount, 1998)

Terry, C.S., *The Life and campaigns of Alexander Leslie First Earl of Leven* (London, 1899) – Includes the accounts of Simeon Ash, Manchester's Chaplain, *A Full Relation …* and *The Diary of Mr Robert Douglas*

Young, Peter, *Marston Moor 1644: The campaign and the Battle* (The Roundwood Press, 1970) – Includes most major sources other than those in Terry and photographs of the de Gomme map and Lumsden's sketch map

General Military Works

Blackmore, David, *Arms & Armour of the English Civil Wars* (Royal Armouries, 1990)

Firth, Charles H., *Cromwell's Army* (Methuen, 1902)

Hutton, Ronald, *The Royalist War Effort 1642–1646* (Longman, 1981)

Roberts, Keith, *Matchlock Musketeer 1588 –1688* (Osprey,2002)

Roberts, Keith, *Soldiers of the English Civil War I: Infantry* (Osprey, 1989)

Roy, Dr Ian, *The Royalist Ordnance Papers 1642–1646 Parts I and II* (Oxfordshire Record Society, 1964 and 1978)

Tincey, John, *Ironsides, English Cavalry 1588–1688* (Osprey, 2002)

Tincey, John, *Soldiers of the English Civil War II: Cavalry* (Osprey, 1990)

Military Manuals

Alexander Leslie, Earl of Leven, *Generall Lessley's Direction and Order for the exercising of Horse and Foot* (London, 1642)

Roberts, Keith, ed, Barriffe, *A Civil War Drill Book* (Partizan Press, 1988)

Tincey, John, ed, John Vernon, *The young Horse-man, or, the honest plain-dealing Cavalier* (Partizan Press, 1993)

Young, Peter, ed, *Militarie Instructions for the Cavall'rie (being a facsimile of the edition of 1632 by John Cruso)* (The Roundwood Press, 1972)

INDEX